The Tenth Inning

Jennifer Staley

ISBN: 0999649507
ISBN-13: 978-0999649503

Twin Publishing, LLC
Farmington, NM 87401

twinpublishing@yahoo.com

DEDICATION

For the already diagnosed families and those yet to come. May you find help amidst these pages but more importantly, may you find *hope*.

CONTENTS

ACKNOWLEDGMENTS

To God for steering this broken and bruised battleship over and through rough waters. You were our constant. Thank You for hearing our prayers.

To Jenna for being my 24/7 sounding board, my go-to girl, my editor, my daughter and most importantly my best friend, thank you! You have answered my every question while helping me understand the value of Google. Thank you for your presence every single day during this process. Your heart and your editing skills are both invaluable.

To my new husband, Eddie, thank you for making me take the summer off to focus on and finish this book. Your encouragement and support of this very important goal of mine has been priceless. Thank you also for taking so much off my shoulders and wanting to take care of me, allowing me to rest.

Thank you to Jordan for your heart and support to both your brother and myself. You brought love and laughter to lighten our load.

My love and gratitude to my parents, Larry and Rosemary Welsh, for teaching me to fight for what I believe in and for giving me a voice – a very loud one at that.

A heartfelt thanks to the Prayers for Justin followers for sending your love and prayers when we needed you the most. I know those prayers pulled Justin through some dark hours.

Thank you to the entire baseball community for taking care of one of your own.

To Tripp and Jayce – I hope this book shows you both that miracles really can happen if you never give up. I love you boys very much!

To all of Justin's friends and teammates – you were the difference. Thank you.

To Jason for your friendship and help in getting Justin through.

Thank you to the doctors and nurses in Houston, Durham and Chicago who went above and beyond every day for Justin and who continue to do so.

To Melissa for being a formatting genius and a generous human being. What would I do without you?

To Shawn for your enthusiasm and expertise in editing this treasure of mine. Thank you for wanting to be a part of our story.

To all of you who put on a fundraiser or donated money for Justin's care. The truth is that we wouldn't have been able to take him where he needed to go without you. Thank you all!

To Justin – your journey is why we are all here. The path you have endured to bring hope to so many others traveling familiar roads is truly a precious gift. Thank you for having such deep faith and for never, ever giving up.

Thank you to all who loved, cared, prayed, thought about, visited, comforted, laughed with, cried with, and fought with Justin. I know we would not be here today without you. I hope someday I can hug and personally thank each and every one of you.

Foreword

To the reader of this book:

 As far back as I can remember, my mother has always been a writer. She has a particularly fascinating way of stringing words together in such a manner that they stick with you and you carry them in the back of your mind for longer than you expect. I think this is partly from her educational background, but also her sensitive soul and feelings that run way too deep. Writing a book was an idea that she tossed around for many, many years, but I think she struggled with content, as most writers do. Stories come from life experiences, and up until a few years ago, she had very little – none that were worth putting pen to paper. And then a lifetime's worth of experience came crashing into her life in a matter of moments.

 This book is pieces of Jennifer's soul on paper - Justin's soul too, some of mine, some of his family and friends', and by the time you're done, you might recognize some of your own in this book. This book teaches how to fight when you have nothing left, how to endure when it seems impossible, how to live bolder every day, how to love with all of your heart, and how to appreciate every moment as if it is your last. These pages accomplish all of these things through a true story written from the perspective of one person who is facing what I presume to be the most heartbreaking thing in the world – watching your child struggle to live every day for many years.

 This story, its lessons, and my mother's words linger with me every day, and if I'm lucky, I'll carry them forever.

--Jenna Solomon

Preface

Journal Entry: July 20, 2011

I have a theory: If you live a troubled life with problems with drugs or alcohol or sex or any kind of criminal activity or problems maintaining relationships then your days will be long on this earth. Why? Because you need to figure your crap out here before progressing. Why else do you think you're here? But if you live a life of moderation and balance, a life of kindness and love, a life of strength and honor then you have other demons to overcome. And what demons are those, you ask? In my opinion, they are usually health related.

And that is what has happened to my son, Justin. You couldn't ask for a better kid, a stronger, more noble child, a more talented athlete blessed with unwavering self-discipline, good morals, outstanding values and a genuine love for his family, his God and his friends. This kid is one of those all-American teenagers, one of those kids who you know is destined for greatness. And then tragedy strikes out of nowhere, literally thin air, left field, whatever description you want to use. And once it strikes, it snowballs and in a month's time you find yourself on a plane headed to meet him at a hospital in Albuquerque and the word "cancer" is actually being spoken. Cancer? What? How? Two months ago this kid was taking home the State Championship in New Mexico for baseball as an All District player. He was rafting in North Carolina and working ropes courses like it was a daily thing for him. He was laughing and playing with his nephew and his sister's dog on the floor at his grandparents' apartment. He was tackling his sister in the pool and begging to eat wings. Then the pain started in his hip and he started losing weight (30 pounds now) and the fevers began. The trips to the ER soon followed, the many tests that no one understood, crutches, pain meds and prayers and now it has come to this. It has come to him, Justin, being admitted to the hospital in Albuquerque with the concern of cancer. It has come to Jenna and I on a plane the first thing the next day to go to him, to love him, to touch his face and to let him know how very much he is loved. And for the first time in my life, it has come to me questioning God. That kid in that hospital bed does not deserve one bit of this - not one bit of the pain or worry or stress or hurt or heartache. But then, does any child?

CHAPTER 1

Justin was as all-American as they come. He embodied the term. His dad is a police officer and I, a teacher. He has an older brother, Jordan, and sister, Jenna, and a dog. Justin loves dogs. He adores his family and has this innocence about him that stayed with him as he grew up. He was rarely sick with "normal" things. I took him to the hospital emergency room a couple of times as a child, once for a respiratory illness, which he was hospitalized for, and once for getting a foxtail caught in his throat, which restricted his breathing. Sure, he had colds now and again but nothing like his brother and sister. He started playing T-ball when he was 4 years old. He was all heart. He fell in love with the sport immediately. Through the years we tried to get him to try other sports just to see if he liked them. We wanted him to be well rounded and to explore all of his options. He played basketball some and was interested in track but track was during the same season as baseball so of course he chose baseball. I remember begging him to just try soccer. He adamantly refused but after much coercion finally gave in. He went to one practice and said "Nope, not for me." He had one love - baseball. That's all he wanted to do, all year long. When he started high school, he fell in with the most amazing group of boys and most of them played baseball. Looking back, I know that God placed each and every boy in his life for a reason - because He knew Justin would need each one of them so much in the coming years. And He knew that they would be able to heal him and help him in a way that no one else and no medicine could.

The summer he was diagnosed, a month before any symptoms set in, Justin went to North Carolina to visit his siblings and his grandparents who were all living there at the time. We went to a ropes course, rafted, visited attractions and swam. Within a week of returning home, Justin started having hip pain. I stayed in North Carolina a little longer to visit with the kids and he called me one day in tears. He said he was in a tremendous amount of pain. I told him to get dressed and I would call his father, Jason, to take him to the emergency room. Justin never complains. He is a strong kid in mind and body. I knew that if he was calling me in that much pain then something must be wrong. He said his left hip was hurting and that he could barely put any pressure on it. I assumed, as did his dad and even the doctors, that it was a sports injury. Justin was constantly working out at that point. He was lifting weights, running and going to baseball practice practically every day. It was only natural that we would assume it was related to his workouts. Jason took him into the emergency room and was sent home with pain meds, which didn't touch his pain. Justin found himself sleeping on the floor trying to find comfort from the agony. When he couldn't stand it anymore, Jason took him back to the emergency room one more time. This time, after blood tests and X-rays, the doctors told Jason that Justin's platelets were low, that he had lesions all over his bones and that he needed to go to the children's hospital in Albuquerque to rule out cancer. The doctor explained that he really didn't think Justin had cancer but it needed to be ruled out. Little did we know that it would be 2 ½ weeks before Justin would leave that hospital in Albuquerque.

That same day, in North Carolina, I was at my parents' apartment when my cell phone rang. It was Jason calling to deliver the news to me. He was letting me know that he was heading down to the Albuquerque hospital right then as a bed had opened up and the doctors said that it was imperative that Justin be brought in right away. He told me what they said about ruling out cancer and I almost wanted to laugh. It sounded like the most ridiculous thing I'd ever heard, but somewhere just beyond wanting to laugh, my pulse quickened and my heart plummeted into my stomach. I sank to the floor and shook. A cry from the deepest part of my gut burst from me and I sobbed. Even though it was against everything I understood, I knew the doctors wouldn't be sending Justin to Albuquerque if cancer wasn't a real possibility. My mind went from being flooded with worry to "What do I need to do?" I called and booked a flight into Albuquerque for the first thing the next morning. Seeing the state I was in, my daughter (Jenna) booked a seat on the same flight as she knew I needed her. I went into the bathroom, dropped to the floor and I spilled a few words onto a piece of paper which became the preface to this book. There was no sleep that night. There were only tears, pain and my mind constantly working, trying to figure out what to do. I had to be medicated. There was no way I was going to make it if I wasn't. It was too much to think about and being away from him made things that much worse. I took a Xanax the morning of our flight. It knocked me out. Jenna let me sleep in the airports and on the planes but would wake me up to get me from one place to another. I don't know where her strength came from, to take care of me when I knew her heart must have been breaking too. That wasn't the last time that Jenna would step up and help out but it was the last time that I would be incapacitated and unable to take care of things.

I knew that what lay ahead of us was huge and I wondered how in the world I would disseminate all of the information to the many people who loved Justin so much. I decided to start a page on Facebook, Prayers for Justin, so I didn't have to answer the countless phone calls, text messages and emails we were already receiving on an individual basis from all the people who wanted to know that Justin was okay. We arrived in Albuquerque at about 10:00 AM and went straight to the hospital and straight to Justin's room. We opened the door to find Justin frail and blue; he was skin and bones. His face was sunken in and his eyes were drooping from the volume of pain meds they were giving him. My heart broke for what would be the first of many times.

CHAPTER 2

When you choose to take on a task like writing this kind of book, you are choosing to visit pain, basically rolling out a welcome mat, by reopening wounds that have otherwise begun to allow time to work its magic.

Soon after we arrived at the hospital, they performed a bone marrow biopsy on Justin. The doctors said we were welcome to stay in the room and watch but that we needed to be seated in case we got queasy. As Justin lay awake on his side with his knees pulled up to his chest, the doctor shoved long, hollow needles into the back of his hip, bending them behind the force of the doctor's weight as he fervently tried to gain access to his marrow. His marrow was so dense that it was a struggle to get the sample but after some time and great will, the doctors slid out of the room with a tube that would forever change us. I will never forget the doctor pulling Jason and me into the hall to tell us that our son had cancer. I remember the way Dr. Sherman looked, standing there at eye level with me with a white beard and glasses. I remember how he looked at us over the top of his glasses as he started saying things about blasts and Pre-B Leukemia, things I didn't understand. I asked him to explain and he said simply, "Your son has cancer. Not only that, but we are seeing a type of cell that we can't identify." I found myself trying to somehow hold onto his words, trying to think about them to make them make sense. In that moment, everything went fuzzy and I could feel my legs begin to buckle as if suddenly the amount of weight they were trying to hold had tripled. I heard nothing else after those words, except my own voice inside my head screaming "NO!" and asking a thousand questions that no one else could hear. Nothing made sense anymore. It had to be a nightmare, it couldn't be real. After all, Justin was the healthiest kid I knew. He treated his body like a temple. He was always in training for baseball so he never ate junk food or drank soda. He worked out all the time and stayed away from drugs and alcohol. Cancer makes sense if you get it from smoking or drinking or too much sun exposure but what had happened to cause Justin to get cancer? I realized that I was shaking and crying. Dr. Sherman asked that we not tell Justin yet, at least not until they could figure out what the other cell was - the one that they couldn't identify.

We knew that we would turn around and tell Justin what the doctor had just explained to us. We had made a pact with Justin; we agreed that anything we knew, he would know. He didn't want to be in the dark about anything. I could absolutely understand that feeling. I wanted to know what the doctors knew, when they knew it. What if I could somehow help or change something or shed light where maybe there was darkness? I had to know because I had to help. Knowledge is power, right? I'd always believed that I could make anything happen in this world that I set my mind to. Couldn't I sway the outcome of this too? If I worked hard enough, couldn't I help keep Justin alive? Maybe that's what Justin was thinking too. This was Justin's health, Justin's life and he deserved to know.

The doctor had just pulled us into the hall so we were standing just outside Justin's hospital room door. I turned and just stared at the door: a door that enclosed Justin, his sister and his grandparents from North Carolina. I wondered how I would open it and find the words to articulate what the doctor had just explained to us moments earlier. As I opened the door, I looked at him lying there with morphine being pumped into him to try and dull a pain that would soon be so deep and so fierce that no amount of medication could touch it. Oxygen was flowing out of a tube into his blue face. He looked so weak. He turned his head to me as I sat next to him on his bed. I held his hand and felt with burning certainty that I would not be able to edge the words past the massive knot in my throat. How would I slide any words out and around that knot? How would I tell him anything? How would I be able to be strong for him? How would I reassure him about something I knew so little about? How would I be calm for him when inside I was a raging tempest of emotions? How do you tell your son that all of his dreams had to be put on hold? How do you find the words to explain that nothing would go as he had planned because *He* had a different plan?

He was in the summer before his senior year and an avid baseball player. It had been his dream to play professional baseball since he was 4 years old. He was supposed to be showcasing that summer for college scouts. He was supposed to use his God given talent to seek out a college that was a match for him but now it seemed that was not God's plan. I sat on the edge of his bed; his legs were over enough that I could sit beside him. I put my hand on his arm and, as his father stood behind me I said, "Justin, you have a type of cancer called Leukemia." He immediately burst into tears and twisted his body in a way that screamed of pain we would never

5

understand, pain that would contort him inside and out and leave him entirely altered. The words that reached up and out of his strained mouth would forever echo in my mind and heart, "I don't want to die. I don't want to leave you." At his age, I never thought about death, about dying. I couldn't imagine what he was going through, the terror that had surely penetrated his heart. What was he thinking? How could I know? Would he tell us? Would he let us in and let us help him? We told him right then that we didn't believe that he would die and that we would FIGHT this with everything we had and we would stop at nothing to make sure he was okay. No one is prepared for that kind of news. All we could do in those initial moments was feel. We couldn't think. We couldn't organize. We couldn't guess or plan or function. All we could do was feel.

"When my mom told me that I had cancer, my mind could only go to one thing and that was death. I laid in that hospital bed thinking, Wow, I'm 16 years old and I am going to die. Because that's what cancer does and that's what cancer is...death." –Justin

Phone calls had to be made. Justin belonged to a baseball team with his best friends in the world, all of whom knew something was going on. He tried to call each one; however with each call, he struggled to find the words and speak them through tears, which in turn made his spleen feel as though it would burst. We had to make him stop calling his friends. We knew they would tell each other. We just needed him to rest.

"I think me saying it out loud and telling people made it real, and at first I didn't believe it. I couldn't believe it." –Justin

We were stunned by how many friends and coaches came to see Justin the following day; his entire baseball team filed into the room, along with a couple of coaches. There was no way that he was allowed that many visitors but the nurses, knowing he needed them, kindly looked the other way. They brought in chairs and gathered around his bed like he was the axle to their wheel.

"I will never forget the phone call I received from Jenn, sobbing, telling me that my best friend had been diagnosed with cancer. I will never forget where I was, the emotions I felt, and that following day. My mother and I drove down to Albuquerque early that next morning to go see him. I remember being so scared to walk into his hospital room. All I could say when I saw him was "Hey Brother," as I was trying to fight back tears, but failing miserably. I remember him starting to cry as well and telling me, "Don't make me cry man, it hurts too much" as he laid there in pain. I remember hugging him and telling him that I was sorry and that everything was going to be okay but not truly knowing if it was going to be or not. I remember it all. I remember it all like it was

yesterday."—Brady Colebrook

We thought that being told that our son had cancer pretty much summed up the situation we were faced with, even though we had no idea what that meant. We thought that cancer equaled chemo for a period of time. We had no idea what kind of chemo or how it would get into his body or what it would do to his body or for how long. We knew he would be sick from it. In the grand scheme of things, we knew nothing. We were so naïve and more scared than we'd ever been in our lives. I feel like I've always been fairly smart but I knew nothing on the subject of cancer. Why would I? I felt like a tourist dropped in the middle of a foreign country with no knowledge of the language or culture. I started researching medical jargon online; just basic terms I'd hear the doctors say. Little did I know that in the following years, I would earn my own degree. It wouldn't be a degree recognized by any hospital or college but rather a degree with a major in perseverance and hope.

CHAPTER 3

It's incredible the things you don't think about - the things that someone has been paid to consider, evaluate and find solutions for. The next day a fertility doctor came in to explain to us that the chemo would make Justin sterile. They wanted to get a sperm sample to freeze so that when Justin was ready, he could still have the option of having children. Thank God someone was thinking. Thank God someone had this covered because we would have never thought of that. We just sat there and stared at the doctor as he explained that he needed the sample rather quickly as Justin would have surgery the next day to place a port in his chest and begin his chemo and he wouldn't be able to give a sample after that. More than anything, Justin wanted to be a father someday. We asked everyone to leave his room and for the first and last time in my life, I offered to look up porn for my son. Still in a great deal of pain and on morphine, Justin laughed a small, drugged laugh and said, "Mom, I know how to look up porn."

Our world changed in an instant. The things I'd never thought I'd say, the thoughts I never thought I'd think, the pain I never knew I could feel, all came to the surface and I found myself almost looking at me from the outside, wondering who I was. As I made sure that Justin had everything he needed, I pulled the door closed behind me and stood out in the hall with a few of Justin's dearest friends. Let me tell ya something, there is nothing like everyone knowing exactly what you are doing to make it extremely difficult in the first place. We all waited and then I went to check on him and noticed his door was open and he was sitting on the side of his bed. Dejected, he said, "I just can't do it." I can't describe the look on his face. What he wanted most, even more than playing baseball, was to be a father. He was devastated. We talked about how God would provide whether Justin biologically fathered children or if he married a woman who already had kids or if he and his wife adopted. God knew his pain and would provide.

As I stared at my youngest child, lying in bed, in so much pain, barely able to open his eyes, I wondered, "How did this happen?"

The Room

Every week the oncologists at the hospital in Albuquerque change for inpatient. This week we were getting a new oncologist, Dr. Stevens. We had only been there for a couple of days and although Dr. Sherman told us that Justin had cancer, we hadn't been given an official diagnosis because they were still trying to figure out the mystery cell that they couldn't identify. Dr. Stevens pulled Jenna, Jason and me into the dreaded "Family Room." It was a room of bad news, a room of pain, a room of tears and loss and fear. He told us he was ready to give us the official diagnosis for Justin: Precursor B Acute Lymphoblastic Leukemia (from here on will be referred to as ALL). Nothing was mentioned about the other cell they kept seeing so I asked him about it. He quickly dismissed my question, saying that it was just an immature normal cell. I knew right then that something wasn't right. Dr. Stevens went on to explain that Justin was considered high-risk because of his age. Children ages 0-10 respond better to treatment; he explained that Justin, at age 16, had a 60%-70% survival rate. Those weren't great odds. How could I even entertain the thought of losing my child? How could I imagine the other 30%-40%? They wanted to start Justin on chemo immediately. His marrow was so dense with cancer cells that he hurt everywhere. His spleen was enlarged from trying to filter them and it hurt Justin to breathe. He was scheduled for a spinal tap, bone marrow biopsy and port placement the next day. The port is a device that is surgically implanted in the chest, with a tube (catheter) that connects the port to a vein. Ideally the tube is connected to the vein just up from the right atrium in the heart. The port would be accessed with a needle and fluids pumped through it into Justin's body. This placement permits chemo to spread throughout his body quickly. Dr. Stevens explained that since he was the oncologist who was on duty when Justin was officially diagnosed, he would be our primary oncologist. He went on to expound on the fact that they had trouble getting the aspirate from Justin's marrow and because of that, they were unable to get his DNA Index, which would help determine if Justin had a more or less favorable prognosis. I couldn't help but feel like red flags were going up all around us. I didn't ignore them; I simply tucked them away until I could get to a place where I could do some research.

Justin went in for surgery the next day for the port placement and bone marrow biopsy. In order to operate on Justin, his platelet count had to be above 50,000 (normal is 150,000-450,000). Platelets are produced in the bone marrow and their job is to clot the blood. Obviously, it's important to have a higher platelet count when doing any kind of surgery so the patient doesn't bleed too much. When they checked Justin's platelets before surgery, they were at 43k. With leukemia patients, the leukemia cells crowd out the normal cells so there is a decline in red blood cells and platelets. Patients often need blood and platelet transfusions to keep them at a maintainable level. They gave Justin a platelet transfusion and checked again and then they were at 41k. The doctors thought that the blood might have been diluted so they drew another set of labs peripherally (directly from his arm, instead of through his IV) and this time his platelets were at 30k. They said they had to get him into surgery because it was critical that they start him on chemo and check his spinal fluid to see if the leukemia was in his central nervous system. I was confused. At that moment I realized our life was going to become a series of choosing between really bad options and hoping and praying we chose the right one. My mind was swimming in uncertainty. How do we make choices between bad and worse? How in the world do we know how to handle that? …and I started to pray.

Now is a good time to explain my personality, I suppose. I'm not one to sit idly by. I don't have a problem speaking my mind or standing up for myself. My dad taught me at a young age to always do so. I'm a fighter. I fight for what I believe and what I want and when my children are involved, there is nothing I wouldn't do. But I would quickly realize that there is only so much I *could* do. It's the most helpless feeling in the world when your child has cancer.

As the doctors were wheeling Justin to surgery, I told them that I wasn't comfortable with them operating on Justin when his platelets were well below the required level and seemed to only be dropping. They consulted with each other and decided to transfuse platelets during his surgery. I didn't even know if *that* would help. We were choosing between risk and risk. On the one hand, if we didn't allow the surgery he could die as the leukemia had occupied his bones and was spilling out into his bloodstream, and we had no idea if it had invaded his brain. On the other hand, he could bleed out and die on the table during the surgery. We were three days in and already the decisions seemed impossible. Dr. Stevens came back to us again and said they would transfuse 2 bags of platelets during the port placement and bone marrow biopsy. Since their major worry was bleeding around the spine during the spinal tap, he said they would check the platelet count before doing the tap. We felt about as comfortable as we were going to get so we agreed, hugged Justin tightly and went to the waiting room. Waiting is the worst! I'm sure we wore a path in the carpet from pacing and I practically ran into the nurse as she was coming out to get us. I will never forget what we saw when we walked back to see Justin. I almost didn't recognize him. His head was bent so far back and his arms and hands were twisted and drawn in on themselves. His legs were bent and he was almost unrecognizable. I stared at him. I looked for remnants of that boy I knew. I looked for his strong jawline, his solid frame and his gentle eyes. My heart broke - again. I immediately started crying and was thankful he was asleep so he didn't see me break down. He looked completely helpless and Justin has always been anything *but* helpless. It took him a long time to come around and when he finally did, he could barely talk. Between his gargled dialogue and motions, we deciphered that he needed to pee so we rounded up a urinal. My son couldn't do anything for himself. He peed on his underwear and on the bed and was upset with himself for not having any control over his body. We reassured him that it was okay, that he was just groggy and we proceeded to clean him up and get clean underwear on him. I knew this was just temporary as he was trying to come out from under the anesthesia and other drugs they had him on but it was incredibly difficult to see him that way.

Although Justin had chemo administered intrathecal (into his spinal cord, carrying it into his brain), during his surgery, his official first day of chemo was the next day. We had no idea what to expect before we researched the various chemotherapy drugs. We knew, generally speaking, that chemo can make the patient throw up and lose their hair but above and beyond that, we had no idea what would happen with Justin. All we did know was that we had no choice. He had no choice. He had to start chemo or he would die. On day one, Justin received Vincristine and Daunorubicin. Online research told us that Vincristine was known for causing constipation, nausea, jaw pain and neuropathy (damage affecting nerves, which may impair sensation, movement, gland or organ function, or other aspects of health, depending on the type of nerve affected). The side effects of Daunorubicin are: nausea, vomiting, diarrhea, sores in the mouth and throat, stomach pain, hair loss and red urine. I can't tell you how many times, throughout this process, that the doctors and nurses told us that only 5% or less of patients experience severe symptoms (aside from nausea). At first I found comfort in that statistic but later I would find horror knowing that with every drug and procedure, Justin fell within that 1-5%. Knowing that these drugs would cause nausea, the nurses gave Justin a 24 hour dose of Zofran beforehand to help combat the side effect. I can still picture the day he started chemo. He was lying in bed, so fragile looking. He had lost so much weight and as heartbreaking as it may sound, the only thing I can compare it to is a victim of the Holocaust. His face was sunken in and his eyes and teeth looked too big for his gaunt and cloudy appearance. His reaction time had diminished and turning to look one way or the other was slow and exaggerated. He was as thin as a rail but that smile - he still had that smile, the one that lit up a room and warmed your heart. It was reassuring to so many. Justin was lying there in his hospital gown, not even tied in the back, and the nurses came in with the chemo and not an inch of their skin was showing. They had on gowns and gloves, masks and hats with a shield that came down over their face. I had to wonder why in the world Justin was so exposed and they were so covered up. It spoke even more of the poison that they had to put into Justin's body to combat the cancer cells. I would later wonder how one body could possibly handle so much pain, so many toxins. The Vincristine was just a 5 minute push, meaning they didn't hook him up to an IV pole. They had a syringe and they pushed it in over a 5 minute period. The Daun took about 30 minutes to give. Justin was severely nauseated but only threw up twice. They gave him a Phenegran/Benedryl cocktail to help with the nausea. I can't believe how sick he had been. On a good note, within hours the chemo relieved him of the unbearable bone pain he had been experiencing for weeks on end.

Over the following week, Justin continued to have intense nausea with some vomiting. He had to have another platelet transfusion but there was a complication. They removed all 3 of his IV's when they put in his port and there are some drugs that cannot go into his port simultaneously. The leukemia in Justin's bone marrow caused him incredible pain which required a great deal of morphine. The doctors had been trying to wean him off but he was still on a substantial amount. To give him platelets, they had to stop his morphine. We didn't realize they stopped it, but after about an hour of being off of it, he had a severe reaction. He started shaking and was extremely nauseated. I called in the nurse, who didn't seem too concerned or move fast enough for my liking. Once we realized they had stopped his morphine, Jason and I kept explaining that we thought it was him withdrawing from the morphine. They finally gave him a morphine boost and Justin immediately calmed down. That was the first of many realizations that I was going to have to be on my game all the time because the nurses and doctors wouldn't always be.

CHAPTER 4

As mentioned previously, I was a teacher before Justin got sick and Justin's dad is a police officer. Justin's diagnosis was just weeks before teachers were supposed to report back to school. Realizing that I would not be able to return when I was supposed to, I knew I needed to find a substitute teacher to fill in for me while I was gone. In my head and as far as I knew from the doctors and nurses, I would probably be out for a couple of months. After looking up everything I could on leave of absence, I discovered that I could be gone until December and have it covered. I know that isn't ideal but neither was the situation we were in. My son had been diagnosed with cancer. Never in any of my worst nightmares would I have thought that to ever be a reality of ours. But there we were staring that reality right in the face and I was doing the only thing I could do. I was going to take care of Justin. There was no question in that. It wasn't an option. The part I had to figure out was how to care for him and keep my job. I talked to a few of my fellow teachers and lined up a substitute who was looking for a long term position. Not long after, I found out that some of the parents of the children in my class were upset about having a long term sub. I was hearing things about them wanting to find someone permanent for my job. There I was, sitting in a hospital night and day with my detrimentally sick child and then I had to worry about job security in addition to worrying about the life of my son. I realized that sometimes things that look like a choice - aren't. In the end, it didn't matter if I had that job or not. All that mattered was Justin. Yes, it was worrisome that I wasn't going to have anything to come back to in terms of a job but then again, was it? On the other hand, Jason's employer was extremely supportive and they were coming together as a unit to figure out how to make the situation easier on him and on us. Things were hard as it was. There were so many issues floating around that needed to be figured out and then there was Justin - his health was all I could seem to think about.

The protocol for Justin's treatment would require 3 ½ years of chemo and from the sound of it, he would be out of school for a while but could return when his counts (blood lab work) were acceptable. When all was said and done, everything changed.

During the 3 weeks that Justin was in the Albuquerque hospital, he had a lot of visitors every single day. People we know traveled down from Farmington. Justin's friends, baseball team and coaches, as well as Jason's and my coworkers all came to see him. In addition to people we knew, there were many people who visited Justin that we didn't know. Baseball players and coaches from areas around the state, church friends of family members and friends of friends all took time out of their day to come visit Justin. It was amazing to see and completely caught us off guard. Word traveled quickly about a teenage baseball player who was diagnosed with cancer and we were flat amazed at how the baseball community all over the world came together for him. Since he was little, all he wanted to do was play baseball. He worked hard every day with the goal of playing in college and eventually the MLB. To have the baseball community pull together like they did and continue to do so, meant the world to him and to us.

"As far back as I can remember baseball filled our weekend schedules. We followed Justin around the country while he played baseball. It was not only his sport, but it was our family's pastime too. Some of his teammates became part of our family and are still as close as family today. One of the hardest parts of this whole experience was knowing we, and Justin, would lose that. He had the potential to play in college, even the pros, but that opportunity was unfairly taken from him. We are all confident he will play again. He was just too good at the game."—Jenna Solomon (Justin's sister)

There was one day in particular when Justin was so sick that he asked to not have visitors. I posted on his Facebook page to let anyone know who may have been thinking of making the 3 hour trip down to see him. I also called some of his friends to let them know but there was a bit of a problem. Justin's baseball buddies were planning on coming down that day to present Justin with his state championship ring that he helped secure months before his diagnosis. I wasn't about to cancel that and I knew by then what those boys did for his spirits and general well-being. No medication could have the effect that his friends had on his health and disposition. I told them to go ahead and come and I let his nurses know but I didn't mention it to Justin. It was going to be a surprise! We let him rest most of the day and the boys came by in the afternoon. Justin lit up when those boys came in. Like I thought, Justin's mood and overall feeling changed nearly instantly. The boys drug folding chairs over and sat all around Justin's bed. It was nothing but smiles on everyone's face. Laughter poured out of the room. A room that moments before was quiet and still, came alive when those 8 boys flooded in to embrace their teammate and friend. I found myself wishing that I could have bottled that day for the upcoming tough ones. They all sat around and joked with him and then a news crew showed up a couple of hours later to do a story on Justin and the boys coming to present him with his state ring. Soon after, smiles and laughter turned to solemn silence. It was hard to see those boys cry as they hugged Justin and said goodbye.

"The 2011 high school season went very well and proved to everyone we were for real and that we were headed in the right direction winning our 2nd state title in a row. Justin Solomon worked his way into the starting line-up by the end of the season and helped us win a ring with his up tempo style and level of physical toughness I was looking for in my players. I was obviously very excited for that group going into the 2012 season. Justin was going to be a senior and he was surrounded by 3 other D1 players. During that offseason something happened that would forever change the faith, the future, and the lives of very many people close to what we were doing. Justin was diagnosed with cancer. I am blown away to this day that Justin was so tough and stronger willed than any human being I have ever witnessed in my lifetime."— Mike McGaha (baseball coach)

After only 2 weeks (I say only but I know that 2 weeks of cancer treatment is a hell that I cannot comprehend) of treatment, it's fair to say that Justin had some tough days, some "done" days, some "I'm not interested in doing this anymore" days. One day he barely made it to the bathroom (he had trouble walking because he was so weak) and he sat on a chair and said, "Mom, what will happen if I just decide that I don't want to do this? It's *too* hard." I looked at him and saw a tear escape the corner of his eye. I couldn't imagine what he was going through, what he was feeling. I looked at him with the love of a mother and reminded him of the intense pain he suffered for a month before and at the time he was admitted to the hospital and explained how the chemo wiped that out. As we were talking, my stomach clenched around a knot and I felt like I might throw up myself. How do you explain to your child that he will die if he doesn't accept the poison into this body that will combat his cancer while nearly killing him? It seemed and seems so surreal. I couldn't believe that my son was so sick. In fact, even now, I find myself picking over everything in my brain and wondering how Justin could have possibly had cancer! As I talked, he just looked at me. I was his momma and I was supposed to protect him, to care for him and I couldn't protect him from this. I told him, I promised him, that it wouldn't always be this way, wouldn't always be this hard. I told him he wouldn't always feel weak or nauseated. Little did I know.

Justin had a very hard time with the dramatic change in his appearance. He had lost so much weight! His thighs were the size his calves had been. He looked frail and…well…sick. We explained that the weight would come back and when he was strong enough, he could work out again and regain his strength and muscle mass. But that didn't stop him from looking down at himself while lying in bed and asking, "When am I going to be *me* again?!" I noticed it too and it made me incredibly angry and frustrated. It made me angry because I felt like cancer was stealing my son from me piece by piece. I felt like I was watching him slowly and painfully disappear. And it frustrated me because he was hurt by how he looked. He had worked day in and day out to get in and stay in great physical condition for baseball. I know he felt betrayed by his body that he had worked so hard to take care of.

CHAPTER 5

When it was time for Justin to be discharged from the hospital in Albuquerque, we were all exceptionally nervous to drive the 3 hours back to Farmington where we were living at the time. We were worried that something could happen or that Justin may have a negative reaction to something and we would be so far away from the one place he needed to be. There was no pediatric oncology care where we lived. Justin was anxious about leaving as well. He knew he was getting exactly what he needed in the hospital and the staff was trained to care for him in his condition. Thankfully, Justin's great grandmother lived in Albuquerque and offered to have us stay with her. She had a 3 bedroom home in a very quiet neighborhood. It would be perfect.

As we wheeled a very fragile Justin out of the hospital in a wheelchair we felt a sense of relief that we would be staying somewhere close by for the next couple of weeks. Justin made it into his grandma's house, into the bedroom and then collapsed on the bed and tried to rest. His rest was fitful as he battled nausea. I decided to sleep with him so I would be close if he needed anything and I could also help him to the bathroom as he was too weak to make it on his own. Everything seemed to have happened so quickly. The decline was unbelievable. The way that the cancer cells depleted him of nutrients, desire, physical appearance and health was both frustrating and infuriating. In a matter of months, Justin looked like a different person. To go the bathroom, I would walk in front of Justin with his hands on my shoulders for support. Every single time we went, which was often because he was so sick, we had to walk in front of a large mirror. And every time, Justin would look over at the body that betrayed him and hang his head. Prayer was something we were so much better at by then. Justin and I would take turns praying at night. It was comforting to know that we weren't alone. For the first couple of weeks since diagnosis, Justin didn't eat but since then his appetite increased and as the days turned into weeks, we watched Justin slowly regain his strength despite his never ending nausea.

We continued to go into the hospital every week for Justin to receive chemo. Everything was a learning process. I cannot express how completely uneducated I was. I knew nothing about cancer and its treatment before Justin got sick. However, I absorbed everything and held onto it - maybe at the expense of other information previously stored in my brain. I didn't care. All I knew or cared about was Justin, his care and getting him better. Every time a doctor spouted off a term or procedure or idea, I researched it. I wanted to know everything. I needed to know everything. I had to know everything.

Our weekly process was an interesting one. We would check in on the clinic floor and have labs drawn to check all of Justin's blood counts and then wait to see the doctor. For a long while, this process consisted of Justin getting a spinal tap once a week. He actually loved the days of spinal taps. He liked the "sleepy milk" (Propofol) that he got to relax as well as the Fentanol. He loved those days so much because after sedation for the procedure, when he first woke up, was the only time he didn't feel sick. After his spinal tap he would go to the 6th floor in another building to receive chemo. I guess when you have something like cancer and so many choices are taken from you, the doctors and nurses try to give you as many choices as they are able. One of his choices on chemo day was a bed or chair. He would almost always choose a bed as he felt terrible all the time. Not that he could ever be said to be comfortable, but he felt best laying down in the fetal position. Occasionally they would have to give him fluids to hydrate him. The various chemos had different effects on him. I guess that made sense. All medications come with a list of side effects; chemo is no different. The one side effect that all chemos seemed to agree on was nausea. Justin was nauseated every single day regardless of how much and what combination of nausea meds the doctors had him on. He didn't lose his hair right away and he wondered often when that day would come.

Justin was an average student and a class clown. He loved to make people laugh. I remember when I would be down or just in need of a good laugh, I would ask him to make me laugh and he didn't hesitate. He was naturally funny and very compassionate. When he was very young, I would get bad headaches and once when he kissed me on the forehead, I told him that he made my headache go away. From then on, he would always kiss me on the forehead to make my headaches disappear. Oh how I ached to have the same effect on him - to be able to kiss his pain away, to be able to kiss him and watch his cancer disappear.

Justin spent his days at his grandma's house watching TV, playing video games and trying to rest. He was so incredibly weak that he couldn't even sit up. His frame was so frail. He walked hunched over dragging his feet, barely the strength to even move them. It was hard to take in, to look at him once strong and virile and see him reduced to skin and bones. His heart though - oh, his heart still beat true. It was just as strong and beautiful as it had always been. He loved his teammates and fiercely missed baseball. We were able to stream the Connie Mack World Series and Justin lay on his side in his bed, as his sister held the computer, and they both watched his teammates play. He was too weak to lift his head but his smile told us all how much he was cheering for them. And we watched him struggle day in and day out. We watched as cancer took and took from him and we also watched as he fought and fought. Justin is a very different kid. He's not the "normal" teenager. He is the kind of person who will stand up for what he believes in. He's honest and has a lost innocence about him. He's a leader. He has a good heart and more will power and determination than anyone I knew.

"Justin is the baby, the little brother, the cute one. He has always been a good kid with a pure heart. He was made to make people laugh. When I heard he was really sick, before we knew the cause, I never thought he would be given the burden of cancer. But now, years later, I know why God put this on him. No one could endure it with the strength and grace that he did."—Jenna

I suppose that's why everyone came together when they heard about Justin's diagnosis. It felt like the world wrapped its arms around us. It was obviously devastating to Justin and even though there is no "good" time to get cancer, it's especially hard to manage when you're a senior in high school and you should be showcasing for college scouts. I've always been told that life isn't fair and while I've always known that to be true, I desperately wished it wasn't this unfair.

After the induction period of Justin's treatment, they did an MRD (minimal residual disease) test. This test showed that Justin was in remission. I don't think I've ever loved the sound of a word more than I loved the sound of "remission". It was time to move to the next phase of treatment, called "consolidation." We mistakenly thought that the induction phase would be the hardest on Justin. We were wrong.

CHAPTER 6

I had numerous issues with the hospital in Albuquerque and the doctors caring for Justin. Justin was considered high risk and was on the most intense treatment protocol. That was fine and it made sense; however, there were so many things that didn't make sense and every time I asked a question of the doctor, he dismissed me and talked to me like I was an idiot for asking. I felt like I had to micro-manage Justin's care. I was completely stressed and worried about Justin on a mental and emotional level. My every thought, my every heartbeat, my every move coincided with the ebb and flow of Justin's well-being. To have to micro-manage every single thing the doctors were or weren't doing just added a level of stress and worry that I didn't feel I should have to concern myself with. Again, my naivety. To those in the cancer world, it may be considered laughable. I would have to watch everything - every single thing the doctors and nurses said and did and what medications they gave him. I had a bad feeling about Justin's care from the beginning at the hospital in Albuquerque. It was something deep, something instinctual. It radiated out to every part of me like a warning. However, after calling around to other hospitals and researching online, I discovered that the treatment for High Risk ALL is very cookbook, meaning that it would be the same no matter where we went. Staying at the hospital in Albuquerque allowed Justin to be closer to that network of friends and family that seemed to make such a significant difference. It also allowed us to go home on the weekends. Those weekends, those moments that Justin had with his friends were the best medicine for him and made more of an impact on his health than any medicine or therapy.

Once Justin started the consolidation phase of his treatment, we stayed at his grandma's house through the week and then went home on the weekends. It was comforting to stay close after treatment in case Justin had any kind of reaction. I remember one particular weekend as we were making our 3 hour drive home, we were both staring out our windows lost in a reverie. I was going over all the data on Justin, every piece of medical history, trying to understand how he could possibly have cancer. I was mad at God. I was so angry as I drove that long, desert road. I couldn't understand how He could allow Justin to have a life-threatening illness. I couldn't understand how any of what was happening could possibly be happening. Then I looked over at Justin, who had just finished another round of chemo. He was drained. He was also staring out his window and I broke the silence and asked, "What are you thinking about buddy?" With great ease, like he was discussing the weather he said, "Oh, I was just thinking about what an honor it is that God chose me to have cancer. It has allowed me touch so many people's lives." I just stared at him for what had to have been 10 seconds before I could say anything, looking from him to the road and back again. I was ashamed of myself. Even as I stared at him, I couldn't understand it. Where did his heart and his faith come from? I set my bitter mind aside as I told him how proud I was of him. It would have been easy for him to be angry. He had so much taken from him so quickly. His plans, his future, his entire life stopped and he was living in a state of limbo. But he was happy. And he was grateful. I wondered if it would ever wear on him, if it would ever catch up to him. I wondered if his heart would ache for a life he planned for but never got to see. I knew mine would ache for him. It already did.

Much of Justin's time at home was spent trying to lead as normal a life as possible. He couldn't be in school because the chemo dropped his counts so low that he could easily get sick. His senior year would be spent distance learning. His teachers emailed his assignments and he would complete them and mail them in or turn them in online if possible. One thing he desperately wanted to do, low counts or not, was go to Homecoming. He had been going to football games and spending time with friends so we decided to let him go to Homecoming and we just prayed it would be okay. He asked a sweet girl, Jimmienell, to go. It did wonders for my heart to see him doing something "normal." He asked her by getting a blank puzzle and spray painting, "Will You Go To Homecoming With Me?"on the puzzle pieces. He kept out the word, "You" and then gave the other puzzle pieces to her teachers to give her in her classes. That same day, Justin went to her house to decorate her room. He bought her a teddy bear and in Hershey Kisses spelled out, "The only thing missing is" and then put down the puzzle pieces that spelled out "you." It was just perfect. It made him happy to do that for her. Justin had never had a girlfriend really. Having been diagnosed with cancer months prior made him feel like maybe he never would, so having that date meant a lot to him.

It's remarkable what we take for granted. For most of us, asking someone to a dance wouldn't be a big deal. To Justin, it was everything. I'm sure he was wondering how many dances he would have left, how many dates he would ever go on. He wanted everything to be perfect.

CHAPTER 7

On September 13th 2011, two months after his original diagnosis, Justin went into the hospital in Albuquerque for a routine spinal tap. Dr. Fisher, a doctor we had only met once before, pulled us aside after Justin's procedure to tell us that he had taken special interest in Justin's case because of the many abnormalities. I just kind of stared blankly at him. I didn't understand what he meant as no one had said anything to us about any abnormalities before. There were things that didn't add up to me but when I brought them up to any doctors, they were dismissed as no big deal. Dr. Fisher walked away to tend to another patient and my mind reeled with questions. When he came back, I approached him and asked what in the world he was talking about. He proceeded to spout off a list of things that weren't "normal," even for a kid with Leukemia: the litic lesions on his bones, the fact that his cells kept dying in culture, they couldn't get his DNA index and the presence of the pro-kin CD 20. I thanked him for taking an interest and doing the research but during the next few days my mind couldn't/wouldn't rest.

I needed to know more so I emailed Dr. Fisher asking for a meeting to discuss Justin's case. We set up a meeting for the following Tuesday. Because Jason and I agreed to always have Justin on the front lines, Justin went with me to Albuquerque for the meeting. The doctor sat us down and explained that Justin's case had some abnormalities, as mentioned before. He said that because they couldn't get his DNA index, they had to do a FISH (Fluorescent In Situ Hybridization) test to see if he was missing any chromosomes. "FISH is a test performed on your blood or bone marrow cells to detect chromosome changes (cytogenetic analysis) in blood cancer cells. FISH helps identify genetic abnormalities that may not be evident with an examination of cells under a microscope."[1] Dr. Fisher explained that they were waiting for the results of that test but basically if the results came back showing that he was missing 2 or more chromosomes, he would need a bone marrow transplant. Dr. Fisher went on to say that Hypodiploidy ALL was a very bad leukemia and it tricked people because it goes into remission right away (as Justin's did) but it always comes back and when it does, it comes back with a vengeance and is nearly impossible to get rid of. "Hypodiploid acute lymphoblastic leukemia is the chromosome mutation of leukemic cells with 45 chromosomes or less. It has been determined that the prognosis of hypodiploid is much less than standard acute lymphoblastic leukemia. The lower the chromosome count, the lower the survival rate."[2] I can't explain how terrifying it is to get the news that your son has cancer and then two months later, get the news that it's a terrible cancer and more invasive action, a bone marrow transplant, may have to be taken. I felt like I'd been punched in the stomach all over again. I couldn't speak as my mind spun around trying to put the pieces together - wondering why the doctors dismissed all the questions I'd been asking when this was why I was asking them. I asked the doctor what he thought, based on what he had seen, about Justin. He answered that he believed Justin would need the transplant and he felt that Justin was missing chromosomes. In addition, he explained that there was an abundance of a certain protein, CD 20, that they were seeing. Dr. Fisher expounded that they would be adding a certain chemo to his regimen to target that protein. I asked what else they would change in his chemo regimen if it showed that he was hypodiploidy and he told me that they wouldn't change anything else. That seemed strange to me since he took a violent shove from high risk to severely high risk. It only made sense in my mind that his chemo would go from intense to severely intense. As Dr. Fisher concluded, he discussed a time frame if Justin did, in fact, need a bone marrow transplant and explained that he would be going to Denver for that as they don't do bone marrow transplants in Albuquerque.

Questions swirled inside my head: How in the hell did any of this happen? How did we get here? How did my son get cancer and how is it so bad that we are talking transplants?? How did our entire world get flipped upside down and would it ever right itself again?

The very next day I got an email from Dr. Fisher. In it, he explained that they got the pathology reports back and our fears were confirmed. Justin was missing at least 6 chromosomes, much more than he thought. He would need a bone marrow transplant. Somehow, in the course of a week's time, we went from Justin needing chemo for 3 ½ years to him needing a bone marrow transplant as soon as possible. Our next step was having HLA typing done on Justin, and soon after Jason and I would have to be typed to see if we were a possible match.

According to bethematch.com, "Human leukocyte antigen (HLA)

typing is used to match you with a donor for your bone marrow or cord blood transplant. This is not the same as ABO blood typing. HLA is a protein – or marker – found on most cells in your body. Your immune system uses HLA markers to know which cells belong in your body and which do not. Half of your HLA markers are inherited from your mother and half from your father. Each brother and sister has a 25%, or 1 in 4, chance of matching you, if you have the same mother and father. It is highly unlikely that other family members will match you. Under very rare circumstances, family members other than siblings may be tested.

About 70%, or 7 out of 10, patients who need a transplant do not have a suitable donor in their family. If you do not have a donor in your family, your transplant team may look for an unrelated donor or cord blood unit for you on Be The Match Registry. When a search is done on the Be The Match Registry, it includes a search of more than 22.5 million potential adult donors and more than 601,000 cord blood units on lists from around the world."[3]

They said they would do the typing a week from the date of that email. I have an unusually close relationship with my children. I'm not saying that other parents don't care for their kids; I'm just saying that my kids are my entire world. There are a lot of things that I can live without but my kids aren't one of them. What do you do? What do you do when your son gets cancer? What do you do when the doctors come back saying it's worse than they thought? What do you do when you find yourself running up against a clock? You do two things: pray and research.

I made phone calls and got online. Sometimes I was talking on the phone while I was looking something else up online. I wanted to know the best hospitals and then I wanted Jason to check with his insurance to see what we could do. I wanted to know if the diagnosis was correct and if the treatment plan up to the point of transplant was standard. I needed confirmation from the best doctors at the best hospitals. I needed to hear other doctors and hospitals tell me that the one in Albuquerque was doing the right thing and the only thing there was to do.

...that isn't what I got.

I called a doctor at a hospital in Houston, Texas that was recommended by a friend of a friend whose daughter had cancer, Dr. Michelle Baker. I was shocked at how easy it was to reach her. I was further shocked by the amount of time she gave me to discuss a patient who wasn't even hers. I told her what the doctors had relayed to me and she agreed with the diagnosis. She then asked me how they had altered his treatment plan. I told her that they hadn't. She said, "Um...oh." I kind of expected that reaction so I asked her what they would do if Justin was at her hospital. She said that they would start him on a highly intense chemo plan, ALL

0031. She went on to say that Justin would be admitted to the hospital for a week, have 2 weeks off for his counts to recover and then be admitted for high dose chemo. She explained that they would continue that until a donor match was found. She then said what I had been thinking, "It only makes sense to move him from intense chemo to highly intense chemo since his diagnosis changed for the worse." I thanked her and said I'd be in touch. She gave me her personal cell phone number and as I text her with more questions I had, she never hesitated to text me back. It was amazing to me - for this busy doctor to take the time to text someone she had never met, someone who may never even come to her hospital. It showed me that she genuinely cared for the children who were so sick regardless of where they received their care. It also stood out to me because I couldn't get the doctors at the Albuquerque hospital to return my calls and Justin *was* a patient there. I called another doctor at another hospital to ask the same questions. This time I called Dr. Mason in Denver, where they were planning on sending Justin for his transplant when the time came. He agreed with what the Albuquerque hospital was doing and had conferred with them on Justin's case, so he was already familiar.

I asked Jason to talk with insurance in case we decided to move Justin. I wanted to be prepared. I didn't want to be held up on an insurance glitch. Jason and I talked extensively about it, we went back and forth. We discussed Justin being far away from friends and family, quality medical care, cost, housing in Houston, insurance acceptance, etc. With the magnitude of this decision we then asked Justin what he wanted to do. He wanted the best medical treatment and went on to say, "I sure hope that money isn't determining where I go for treatment. I want to go to the place that's going to make me okay." We continued to talk about it and pray about it.

I felt it though. I knew in the back of my mind that we needed to move Justin to Houston. In fact, I didn't think we had any other choice. What if we didn't and something happened? I'd never forgive myself. It wasn't worth the risk. Jason and I decided to talk to the hospital in Albuquerque and ask them why they didn't follow the same protocol as the one in Houston. We went down the following Monday for chemo but Justin's counts were too low so we had to wait until the next day. They cancelled chemo the previous week because Justin's counts hadn't recovered yet. That was going to be the 3rd week that Justin was off chemo so I was concerned. The doctor said for us to come in the very next day, a Tuesday, for HLA typing and they would run his labs then to see if his counts were high enough for chemo.

In the meantime, I contacted Dr. Baker at the Houston hospital to tell her that I was almost positive that we were coming and would be there the following Monday to begin treatment. Yes, it may have been a bit presumptuous but things were shoving us in that direction. I chose the following Monday because Homecoming was Saturday and Justin was feeling great and looking forward to it. I figured that we would leave around 2:00 AM Sunday morning when he got home. I knew it was an 18 hour drive so we would have to leave as soon as possible to get there and be ready to go Monday morning. I was worried, okay? I was worried that Justin currently was at a hospital with doctors who didn't know what was best for him. I was worried that he would get behind where he needed to be in treatment and I was terrified of that ticking clock. They said the cancer would come back, that it almost always comes back. But when would it come back? I felt like we had to move quickly to do everything we could to keep it at bay until we could get Justin his bone marrow transplant. Dr. Baker agreed to us arriving then and explained that we would go to clinic for Justin to have his port accessed and get labs, then to PACU (Post Anesthesia Care Unit) for a spinal tap and triple chemo and then Justin would be admitted. She said *not* to let him have chemo that week at the hospital in Albuquerque as they needed him in tip top shape. She also told me that I needed to gather all of Justin's medical records and scans. Since we were mostly positive we were going to leave, I ran around and gathered his records, which was no easy task as he had been to several places before the initial diagnosis and had records everywhere.

That next day we went back to the Albuquerque hospital for our and Justin's HLA typing. We informed the nurses at that time that we were going to take Justin to Texas. One nurse in particular seemed shocked and honestly put out. She said we would need to speak to Dr. White, Justin's now primary oncologist, to let him know. We switched Justin's primary oncologist a month prior as I was frustrated with the lack of communication with Dr. Stevens. I had no problem talking to Dr. White as I wanted to handle things the right way. Not to mention, I knew that once Dr. Baker told me not to let Justin get chemo that week, I would have to let them know our intentions. I went on to ask for any notes or scans they had so I could take them with us to Texas. When asked why we were taking Justin to a different hospital, I explained that since Justin took a violent shove from high risk to severely high risk, I felt that his protocol should reflect that. The Albuquerque hospital wasn't going to change anything and the Houston hospital would do things differently. My biggest concern was keeping the cancer at bay until he could be matched with a bone marrow donor. I felt that the chemo would have to be stepped up to make that happen. Soon after, we had social workers stopping by. One lady asked me what they would do differently at the Houston hospital and I told her that they were going to start Justin on ALL 0031. She left only to come back to tell me that they would be opening up the ALL 1131 protocol there the following week. Well, that wasn't the protocol I was referring to but she insisted it was because ALL 0031 was older and was closed. I knew that but some things work and apparently that protocol had more success even if it was older. I reflected on that for a while. Why does everything need to be replaced? What if older things work? Just because something is older doesn't mean it doesn't work as well. And then I felt even more certain that I wanted to take Justin to a different hospital. I needed us both to be around doctors and people who understood that concept.

When Dr. White arrived he pulled us into a small meeting room. Over the past month, I had left several messages for this man to call me and he never did - not once. As we all sat around a large wooden table, he asked what was going on and I explained that I'd been talking to an oncologist at the hospital in Houston and we were going to move Justin. I told him about the treatment plan they were going to put him on and how it only made sense to me. It didn't make sense to me that a doctor would continue with the same protocol given the new information. It felt almost "lazy" to me. Dr. White said that they could do that there in Albuquerque if we wanted.

It was shocking to me how much the doctors wanted to listen to me then and how they were willing to let me call the shots! Not that I had any confidence in that hospital but if I did have any, it was right at that exact moment that it would have gone out the window. Yes, I'm a mother and my son's biggest advocate. Yes, I did heaps of research and talked to several other doctors but I'm *not* a doctor. I'm a mother. I couldn't understand why the doctors had no conviction. I didn't get why they didn't stand by what they believed in. Then I wondered if they believed in anything or if they were there for the almighty dollar and to hell with what my son actually needed. I absolutely didn't want to be recommending to our oncologist the best course of cancer treatment for our son. I didn't want to have to micro-manage his healthcare and be doing research on the side so I could tell the doctors how to do their job. I wanted to be Justin's mother. I wanted to focus on loving him while the doctors did what they were supposed to do. It was in that fleeting moment that I knew God was reassuring me that we were making the right decision.

Dr. White went on to explain how costly it would be to move Justin to the hospital in Houston and that there was, "no sense in it." I wasn't comforted by what he said but I listened. He said he would call Dr. Baker, find out what she was planning and see what they could do there. He kept harping on the fact that we were going to be paying hundreds of thousands of dollars to take Justin to Houston. How much would you pay to keep your child alive? I didn't care how much it was going to cost. I would have gone anywhere for any amount of money if it meant saving my son's life. When I first started talking to the doctor at the Houston hospital, she told me that all cost had to be paid up front. There was no "making payments." Naturally, it worried us. We weighed so many options but cost really wasn't one. We would figure it out. We had to. There simply was no other choice. Justin's life was on the line and I wasn't willing to risk it just to cut cost. How much is peace of mind worth and what is the value of your child's life? Jason was still trying to figure out if our insurance would accept the hospital in Houston as in-network. Jason was on the fence as to whether or not we should take Justin to Houston. I was adamant about taking him there. Justin was, "Take me where I will get better and don't let insurance be an issue." Finally I said, "Okay, let's lift cost up and out of the equation. Now, where do we go?" On that note, everyone agreed on the hospital in Houston. We all slept well that night and the next morning I called Dr. Baker. I told her that we were 100% sure we would be there the following Monday. She said that sounded great but then went on to ask, "By the way, was that doctor ever going to call me?" I was shocked. Dr. White had never even called her. After all of this arguing and all of the fuss, he never even made an effort. I was disgusted.

Dr. Baker then suggested that we take Justin to a sperm bank to have his sperm frozen because the upcoming intense chemo, radiation and preparation for a bone marrow transplant would definitely leave him sterile. I thought it was too late to do that but she assured me that it may not be and we should try. We were still in Albuquerque from our other appointments so right when I hung up with her, I called the hospital in Albuquerque and left a message to cancel our meeting with Dr. White and then I immediately called the sperm bank at the hospital to see if we could get Justin in that day. Keep in mind that this was a Wednesday and we were trying to get everything figured out and accomplished before the weekend as Justin was planning on going to Homecoming that Saturday and then we intended on leaving for Houston the minute he came home from Homecoming. Justin's sister, Jenna, was flying in that very day to help us drive to Houston and to help me with things for a while. She was originally supposed to start her college classes but upon Justin's diagnosis, she changed her courses to online so she could be there for me and her brother.

Some moments in time define us. Maybe not entirely but they lead to a defining of ourselves. I believe that Justin's illness did that for many people, me included. I know it was the beginning of another path for Justin's brother and sister. Jenna was 18 when her brother was diagnosed with cancer and for the following 4 years, she would show complete selflessness when it came to him. Jordan was 20 and made Justin a priority, making sure to see him and talk to him as much as possible.

Okay, where was I? Oh yeah - sperm bank. They agreed to have Justin come in to see if he had any active sperm. Nothing like picking up your daughter from the airport and heading to the sperm bank. My gosh, the roads this journey led us down - the way we were ripped open and sewn back together with God's grace.

We signed in at the andrology clinic and Justin went to take care of things. It was a little weird sitting out in the waiting room knowing what Justin was up to behind closed doors. It was a little weird for him too, to take care of things knowing we were all sitting out there waiting for him. After Justin finished, he came out in the waiting room with us and fell asleep on the floor. That was a laughable moment for us. We all high-fived when the tech came back saying that Justin had active sperm and they froze 3 vials. We learned that they can keep the vials for up to 10 years and we have to pay a quarterly storage fee. We were grateful that Dr. Baker suggested that we have his sperm tested again to give him the chance to biologically father children.

With the decision to take Justin to Houston, we drove back to Farmington with Jenna in tow. Having decided to take Justin to Houston, we had to figure out what to do about his schooling. It was his senior year and he had the most amazing group of friends. I knew he would want to try to graduate with them and walk with them on graduation day, but it was still a conversation we needed to have. Justin was adamant about working on school work from Houston so he could graduate with his class, so we met with his teachers and the principal to try to figure out how to effectively make that happen. Thankfully, Justin had a great group of teachers and an amazing principal - all of whom were on board and wanted to help Justin through the process. We devised a plan to get him to graduation and then came up with ways to execute said plan. We were deeply thankful that they all wanted to help Justin so much!

CHAPTER 8

Homecoming was approaching quickly. Some great friends of ours, Christy and Clay Jaqua, offered up one of their limos for Justin to use. It was shaping up to be a fairytale evening. Justin was able to ask 3 of his friends and their dates to join him in the limo. As luck would have it, his date's mother is a photographer and she took pictures of the kids that were absolutely amazing. Jenna and I went with her to take the pictures. We had such a great time, laughing nonstop. Justin had obviously already started chemo and you could see some of the effects on his appearance but my gosh, still nothing could touch that smile. He was so happy in that moment and life seemed "normal" again. I stood back and watched him as tears slipped from underneath my eyelids. A smile spread across my face and I realized we had *that* moment. We were living in it - there were no doctors or needles or medication or tubes or procedures. There was only then and we were laughing and smiling and happy and life didn't seem so dark and scary and terrifying. And I was thankful. It would be sometime later before I realized that we would live our lives in so many of those moments in between. Jenna and I watched as the group climbed into the limo and then she and I ran around town trying to handle last minute things and get back home to finish packing for our trip to Houston. We would leave as soon as Justin got home from the dance. It was going to be a long couple of days. It was hard on my heart because as wonderful as it was to see Justin happy doing "normal" things, I knew I would have to jerk him away the minute he got home. I would have to take him away from the only home he knew and the best friends in the world to a foreign place with more things we didn't understand. The immediate future would hold a great deal of pain and solitude.

The Justin that we saw being carried off by a limo was not the same Justin that came back from the dance around 2:30 AM. This Justin was grim and sad. He had a look in his eyes of heartbreak and longing for a place he would soon be without. The car was packed, the GPS was charged and we loaded into two vehicles to embark on a journey that would change us entirely.

It was 3:00 AM. Jason had to drive a separate vehicle as far as Albuquerque, 3 hours down the road, as he would need a vehicle after flying back from Houston. Jenna, Justin and I piled into the Jeep Grand Cherokee and picked up Jason in Albuquerque. We arrived in Houston Sunday evening and checked into a hotel a good friend booked for us. Our plan was to try to get our accommodations figured out at the Ronald McDonald House the following day. It didn't take long for us to crash as we were exhausted from the trip and had an early appointment set for the next morning.

We had to be at the Houston hospital at 7:15 AM. As we turned onto Fannin Street in the middle of downtown Houston, in the dark, we were completely intimidated. The hospital was lit up and so menacing. There were so many buildings in the medical complex and bridges to connect them. On a whim, we guessed at a building and it was a lucky guess. After arriving on the 14th floor, Justin slunk onto a couch with a look that spoke of exhaustion but also of heartbreak. Here he was, miles and miles away from the place he called home and the friends he had come to love so dearly. His sister and dad were with us for the moment but soon enough, everyone would leave and it would be Justin and me in this big city with its enormous, intimidating hospital and no friends or family for hundreds and hundreds of miles.

Justin's port was accessed and then we met Dr. James. Dr. James is a colleague of Dr. Baker and was simply reviewing all of Justin's paperwork. I gave her the 3 large packets of Justin's medical records and 2 DVD's of scans. She left and returned not 10 minutes later with a good overall idea of Justin's journey. I was shocked. I couldn't believe that she had filtered through all of that information in such a short amount of time and was able to make sense of it. We hadn't been there long and I was already impressed. From there we went down to the 7th floor for a spinal tap. They didn't let us watch as they had in Albuquerque. That was somewhat tough for me. It takes a lot of Propofol to get and keep Justin under while they do procedures like spinal taps and bone marrow biopsies. I explained that to the doctor and made my way out of the room. We went to get Justin a sandwich so he would have something to eat in recovery when he woke up. When they called us back to see him, I couldn't believe how spacious the recovery room was. There were 24 beds where there were only 3 at the hospital in Albuquerque. Justin was going to be admitted to begin his intensified chemo regimen so we had to wait for quite a while in recovery for a bed to become available. It was around 5:00 PM before Justin was in the room where he would reside for the week.

It took some getting used to; all of it did. It all seemed like a whirlwind – from Justin's diagnosis to beginning chemo right away to then receiving a different and scarier diagnosis of a rare form of leukemia, to moving 17 hours away to live in a distant city while receiving enough chemo and eventually radiation to take Justin to death's door and then drag him back in preparation for a bone marrow transplant. We were there. We were in for the long haul so we settled in and got as comfortable as we could, knowing this was still very much only the beginning.

I stayed with Justin every single night. Jenna and Jason got checked into the Ronald McDonald House which was just up the road. The doctor said that the chemo Justin would be getting was very intense and his counts would bottom out. The week he was released they wanted him in for counts twice. Jason went back to New Mexico and Jenna stayed in Houston with me until almost Thanksgiving. We took him in but his counts never got that low. Through everything thus far, there was only one time that his counts truly bottomed out and that was after the dreaded chemo, Ara-C.

The following week we went to a Texans football game, courtesy of the Ronald McDonald House. The RMH always had tickets to one thing or another, which helped significantly in our quest to stay busy. My goal was to keep Justin active when he was out of the hospital. There wasn't a TV in the room at the RMH, so we bought a little 24" TV so Justin could play his video games. We also bought *The Big Bang Theory* to give him something to watch. I worked hard to keep him from slipping into depression. I didn't want him to have too much time in his own head. Jenna and I took him to the zoo and the aquarium as well as a hockey game. There were days when he didn't feel like doing anything and he would just lie in bed and try to sleep off his symptoms. Brady, his best friend, surprised him around Halloween. Jenna went to pick him up at Hobby Airport and I told Justin she had to go to the store to get some personal items and would be back soon. Justin had no idea that Brady was coming.

We were killing time at the RMH and there was a knock on the door. Justin was annoyed by Jenna taking so long and he yelled to her, "You have a key!" I told Justin to open the door and to stop being mean. He walked over and jerked the door open and standing there was Brady. Justin couldn't believe it. His hand flew over his mouth and then Brady and Justin hugged. It was exactly what Justin needed. There were times all throughout Justin's journey when I would call one of his closest friends and ask if there was any way they could visit. It was hard on Justin to be ripped away from them. They were all seniors and his buddies were living the life that Justin always pictured living right beside them. He couldn't and it sucked. There's just no other way to say that! Jenna and I did everything we could to keep Justin's spirits up but sometimes it was all just too much. Having a visit from one of his closest buddies often made all the difference. We swooped up Brady and all went over to the Galleria to look around and eat some lunch. On Saturday, we drove to Galveston, Texas and spent the day on the beach. It was a great day. We took Brady to the Texans game on Sunday and afterwards went to Buffalo Wild Wings to eat. Monday was Halloween and we were lazy during the day but that night we went to a Haunted House. Justin's spirits were lifted for 5 days. He felt somewhat normal doing things with his friend.

Eventually Tuesday came and Brady had to leave. Justin was readmitted to the hospital for another round of chemo, this one even more intense than the last. This was another of those "moments in between" and we were coming to realize how important those moments really were. We kind of adopted the motto "to live in the moments in between." We knew to absorb every moment when we were out of the hospital and to love each other more fiercely. We came to understand the adage, "living on borrowed time." Brady accompanied us as we waited for Justin to get his spinal tap. He was in recovery with us when Justin woke up and he went up with us to Justin's room when he was admitted. It was heartbreaking to watch them hug and say goodbye. Justin's upcoming week was going to be grueling. He was scheduled for high dose Methotrexate as one of his chemos. It took 24 hours to administer and then at the 42 hour mark they had to give him a drug to reverse the effects. The Methotrexate kills folic acid, which is instrumental in creating red blood cells. It also prohibits the cancer cells from replicating. In addition to the Methotrexate, Justin would get high dose Ara-C (the drug that bottomed out his counts and made him feel horrible). Before, he got 75 mg of Ara-C a day for 4 days. This time he would get 12,000 mg a day for 2 days. I was worried given how he handled the much lower dose. I figured that if anything would kick his butt, it was that.

We settled in and waited. Some of the side effects of Ara-C are flu like symptoms and he got that in spades. He covered up his head with his blankets when the effects really set in. He was achy and started running a fever. They had to start him on antibiotics to be sure he wasn't getting sick. He felt terrible and moaned in misery. He ended up asking for Phenergan for nausea and to help him sleep it off. They stopped the Ara-C on Friday and by Saturday morning he was feeling much better! He also knew that our friend, Christy Jaqua, was flying in to see us. I left Jenna at the hospital with Justin and went to the Ronald McDonald House to shower and wait for Christy and Jimmienell (the girl Justin took to Homecoming). We were excited about the surprise for him. I knew it would make him feel better right away. We got back to the hospital and Christy and I went in to see Justin. He was happy to see her. He was sitting on the edge of his bed when the door opened and a cute, blonde girl came in asking for directions to the bathroom. Justin had to do a double take and about came out of his skin when he saw that it was Jimmienell. They immediately fell into their routine of fun and goofiness. Justin was scheduled to be discharged that day and when we finally left, we went over to the RMH and then to grab some lunch at Jason's Deli. Justin wasn't feeling great. He seemed to *always* be nauseated anymore. Eating was hard. Walking around was hard. Talking was even hard sometimes. He felt his most comfortable laying down in the fetal position. He refused to do that though - not with his friends there. Justin didn't eat lunch but he sat with us and we talked about what we wanted to do that night. We opted for going to the Galleria and going ice skating. Again, something I was worried about for Justin because I knew he didn't feel well but I also knew he wouldn't miss out on this time for anything. We went back to the RMH first to change and upon walking in, I was handed 5 tickets to the Taylor Swift concert. I took the tickets to the group and asked if they wanted to go ice skating or to see Taylor Swift. Jimmienell screamed with excitement when I said Taylor Swift so I knew where we were going. Before walking out the door, Justin threw up one last time for good measure. He was ready to go. We made it to the concert and it was quite the ordeal. I didn't realize what a big deal Taylor Swift was until we were at the concert. The kids had a good time and we no sooner walked in our room at the RMH and Justin threw up again. I knew he felt awful at the concert. He was pale but his smile was still bright. He refused to leave. He was exactly where he wanted to be doing exactly what he wanted to be doing. I couldn't argue with that.

The following day we had plans to go to the Texans/Browns football game. We were all excited and although Justin still wasn't feeling great, he was feeling better and definitely wanted to go. He still had a lot of nausea and fatigue but it was almost as though he was absorbing it; taking it in as a necessary evil but wasn't about to let it dictate how he lived his life. Justin was showing cancer who was really in control. The game was great and we followed it again with dinner at Buffalo Wild Wings. The next day we all went to Kemah, TX on the coast. We rode a painful, wooden roller coaster, walked on the boardwalk, ate at Joe's Crab Shack and enjoyed being outside living! It was another amazing visit with friends. However, similar to the visit with Brady, it had to come to an end. The following day Justin was admitted again for chemo and Christy and Jimmienell had to leave. About a week after they left, it was time for Jenna to leave as well. She was such a wonderful help! The night Jenna left Justin was admitted to the hospital again, this time for neutropenia and a fever. "People with neutropenia have an unusually low number of cells called neutrophils. Neutrophils are cells in your immune system that attack bacteria and other organisms when they invade your body. Neutrophils are a type of white blood cell. Your bone marrow creates these cells. They then travel in your bloodstream and move to areas of infection."[4] So basically, Justin could get sick easily. They kept him for 4 days while they did cultures and had him on antibiotics to help in case he had an infection. We knew though, that it was side effects of the chemo. Justin had his "normal" weeks of admittance to the hospital for chemo so it was extra awful when he was hospitalized for bad side effects and possible illnesses during his in between weeks.

A few days after discharge, my parents arrived from North Carolina. Their plan was to stay through Thanksgiving. I knew right away how absolutely critical it was to Justin's physical health to keep his mental health in check. I knew he would need people. I knew that more than any medication or treatment or doctor or hospital, he would need the people he loved and who loved him so much. I knew it would make all the difference. That's why I tried to plan friends and family visits in waves. That didn't always work as Justin often ended up in the hospital at unscheduled times. I tried to arrange it so people came on holidays or when Justin wasn't in the hospital and that they came at different times. The difference the visits made was noticeable. Justin's spirits were lifted and he floated on that high as long as possible before he came crashing back down. Sometimes the lows after a visit were even lower because he remembered exactly what he was missing.

Before Justin was readmitted for another round of chemo, we had a great visit with the family. Justin went back into the hospital right before Thanksgiving. That was the first of many holidays spent inpatient and it was one of the hardest days yet. My parents and brother were there with us but it just wasn't the same. Justin's older brother and sister were back in North Carolina cooking a Thanksgiving meal for our family there and we missed them all terribly. It just didn't feel like Thanksgiving. We all sat around in Justin's hospital room and watched TV. Late that evening some people we met in Farmington who lived in Houston brought us some of their Thanksgiving meal. It was thoughtful and kind of them. That was the beginning of new friendships.

My parents left on December 1st and Justin's dad arrived (again - the whole wave theory). I'd been having a lot of sharp pain in my stomach and had an appointment the same day to be seen. It's funny how life just doesn't stop. Life doesn't think, "Oh I'll wait…they are dealing with some pretty big stuff right now." It just keeps on pushing and pulling and somewhere amidst it all you have to find some sure footing and dig in. I found out that I had gall stones. The doctor I saw wanted to remove my gall bladder the following week. I'd had some bad attacks since we got to Houston so I agreed. Plus, it helped that Jason was there at the time to help with things. On Dec. 5th, Justin was admitted in the middle of the night for fever and neutropenia. It was another 4 night stay with antibiotics and blood cultures. That was the protocol and it was getting to be routine. The antibiotics were because of the fever. Even though the fevers were more than likely chemo fevers, they had to be sure they took care of any infection that could be lurking about. They ran blood cultures, mostly to be sure there was no infection in the line in his chest but also to check for other infections. My surgery was scheduled for the next day and I almost cancelled it but I knew it would be a problem down the road if I didn't just have it taken care of and Jason was there to help so I just went with it. I walked over to a different hospital in the morning, had the surgery and went back and stayed with Justin. I was in a lot of pain but I had to be there for Justin. He slept on the bed and I slept on the couch as per our routine the past 5 months. Justin was still running a fever but nothing was showing up in his cultures. For that we were thankful.

CHAPTER 9

We were thankful that day for something else as well. We got the phone call, the one we waited on from the moment we knew that Justin needed a bone marrow transplant and had his testing done. It was a woman on the other end of the line, stating that they found a perfect (10/10) match for Justin. They told us they had some other tests to do but Justin should be ready for transplant by the end of the month, a true Christmas miracle. That news carried us through the next 2 weeks. On December 19th, Shane and Ray, two of Justin's closest friends, came to surprise Justin. Justin was at the Houston hospital that entire day for chemo and I snuck away to pick up the boys from the airport. When I returned with the boys, Justin was laying on a couch, with his back to me, feeling sick. We snuck up on him and I said something to him to make him roll over and look at me. To his surprise, Shane and Ray were standing there. Justin jumped up with such a big smile on his face. I have seen smiles - bright smiles even. That smile of Justin's when friends and loved ones came to see him was the brightest. Justin hugged his friends tight and just like that he felt so much better. I'm telling you, Justin's friends and family and foremost God are what kept this kid alive. I believe that. As I'm sitting here typing this with tears in my eyes, I know it to be true.

The boys got a hotel right by the hospital and Justin went and hung out with them that evening. As I was dropping him off I asked him if he was going to be okay. He looked at me and said, "Are *you* going to be okay, Mom? We've been together, nonstop, for 2 months." Oh, how I adore him. It was true. Maybe I was going to have a harder time than him. I called him a couple of times to check on him and he was happy to be doing something normal without doctors and even without me. I was thrilled that he was getting to be with his friends. I knew Justin's reaction to the chemo. I knew he would try to put on a face for his friends that he felt better than he actually did. And that was okay if it was what he wanted. I know he appreciated the time with me because he could just let go and be sick. He could moan and throw up and lay in the fetal position for hours on end and not worry about being upbeat and happy when maybe he didn't feel that way. I know his friends would have understood if he did those things with them but he didn't want to and maybe he even felt somewhat better and didn't need to.

We had such a great visit with Shane and Ray. The next day we all went to a hockey game, to eat wings and to the Galleria. While at the Galleria, I received a phone call that broke our hearts. Justin's bone marrow transplant doctor called to tell me that Justin's donor fell through. My heart fell. I was listening to her and watching Justin laughing with Ray and Shane and wondering how in the world I was going to tell him. Apparently, the donor had second thoughts from what I could gather during the phone conversation. I felt sick and scared at the same time. The doctor went on to explain to me that they were moving onto the next match to try to get clearance. This match wasn't a perfect match like the other one had been but was 9/10. She said they were hoping to only be pushed back a week. I hung up the phone and looked at Justin with terror. He asked me what was wrong and I explained to him what my phone call was about. It was like someone punched him in the stomach. He immediately had to sit down. Bone marrow meant life for Justin. He knew he needed it to survive and it was such a miracle when we got that initial phone call weeks before saying that he had a perfect match lined up. This recent news crushed Justin. I can't imagine how it made him feel, how it scared and worried him. I saw a look in his eye similar to the one I'd seen when he was first diagnosed: fear of dying. I'm thankful that Shane and Ray were there. I felt like they somehow helped him deal with the news a little better.

December was a great month for visits. Jenna, Jordan and Tripp (my 1 year old grandson) flew in for Christmas and Shane and Ray weren't scheduled to fly out until the next day. Between the lot of us, I don't know who was more excited about their visit. I fell in love with my grandson, Tripp, before he was ever born and I missed that kiddo like mad. I picked them all up at the airport and let me tell you how hard it was to not grab Tripp and squeeze and kiss him. He was so adorable but I knew he probably didn't know who I was as I hadn't seen him in so long. He just kind of stared at me, not quite sure what to think. Justin was at the hospital getting outpatient chemo. His dad was with him and Shane and Ray walked over to the hospital from their hotel. There were so many of us there supporting Justin that we took up an entire back room. Justin was thankful and very happy. That night we all went to Fuzzy's Pizza and just enjoyed and appreciated each other's company.

Upon returning to the RMH, someone with administration told me that we would have to check out for a while because we had been there so long. I didn't quite know how to process that. I mean, we weren't there for fun. We weren't just hanging out *and* we were even paying to stay there - $25 a day. Justin was scheduled to go in for his transplant in a matter of weeks so it was obviously a terrible time to not know if we had a place to stay. When I brought that to their attention, they still insisted that we had to leave. We were frustrated but decided we would leave for a week when Justin was admitted for his bone marrow transplant since we would both be staying at the hospital anyway.

Shane and Ray left the next day and my brother, Kevin, flew in to spend the holidays with us. Even though we were at the Ronald McDonald House, we were all together and I think we all appreciated each other a bit more. Christmas was wonderful! Not only were we not supposed to have a TV in our room at RMH but we weren't supposed to have a Christmas Tree either. I, however, couldn't go without a tree. I wanted Justin to have a real Christmas with a tree and presents underneath. And that's exactly what we had. There were gifts under a beautifully decorated tree and there were plenty of people in our room that you couldn't really walk around in it at all. Kevin was staying at a hotel but everyone else was staying at the RMH with Justin and me. Jenna and I attempted to make Christmas cookies with Tripp in the community kitchen at the RMH. We had our own shelf in a very large refrigerator as well as in a cabinet for our food but it's very difficult and uncomfortable to cook in such an unfamiliar area with so many other families around. We made the best of it, of course, and the facility was very nice. It wasn't home although it was our home for a while.

We got a Christmas present on Christmas Eve. I received a phone call from Hospitality Apartments. They told us that they had an apartment come open and we could move in on December 30th. I couldn't believe it. The apartment was even better for Justin since he was going to be immune suppressed after transplant. He would need a place where there were no other sick kids. It was a one bedroom with twin beds, a kitchen and a living room. They even had cable. When your life takes a turn and you are living in either the hospital or the Ronald McDonald House for months on end, things like your own space and cable mean quite a lot!

Tripp started to get sick and then shared with Jenna and me. The three of us slept in the same bed to try to keep anyone else from getting it. I got the worst of it. Though I felt bad, I wasn't going to miss out on the family festivities. I just made sure to stay away from Justin. The day after Christmas we all went to a hockey game, Tripp's first, and it was a blast. The day after that, the kids had to leave. The disappointment in seeing them go was in direct proportion to the happiness we felt when they arrived. By the end of the month, December 30th, all of our company was gone as it was time for my brother to go home as well.

On January 3rd, we spoke with doctors at another hospital in Houston about the total body radiation that Justin would be receiving prior to transplant. Talk about scary stuff!! They talked to us about all of the possible side effects, stating that the more extreme would only happen in 1%-5% of patients. You know how you always want your child to be unique and stand out? Justin was so unique that he would almost always fall in that window of 1%-5% of patients who would get the brunt of nearly every side effect. The doctors explained how they would make iron casts of Justin's lungs to try to block most of the radiation from hitting his lungs. I sometimes just kind of stopped in my tracks and zoned out as the doctors talked like they were dictating a grocery list - something they did regularly. It was another day for them but for me and Justin they were talking about life and death. And again, I wondered how we ended up there and I questioned - I always questioned every single decision I made because how could I not? But even as I was questioning everything I knew that I didn't think I had much of a choice. Not really. It was, "He will die if he doesn't have this" versus, "He could die anyway." How does anyone make a choice like that? You make the best decision you can with the information you have. The doctors don't talk like that though. They don't talk to you like it's even a choice because to them, it isn't.

On January 5th, we were still waiting to hear if the second donor was going to work out. There were still tests that needed to be completed. Justin was scheduled to get his port removed on the following Monday and to have a PICC (peripherally inserted central catheter) line placed in his arm sometime after. He was also scheduled to have a few more tests that next Tuesday to be sure he wasn't sick with anything (no matter how small) as it could kill him since he wouldn't have an immune system once things got underway with the conditioning. The conditioning is all the chemo and radiation they would give him to completely destroy all of his bone marrow so they could then go in and replace it with healthy marrow that would make healthy cells. He was tentatively scheduled to be admitted the next Friday and begin his conditioning. In the meantime, we waited. Waiting was hard. I've never been a patient person but this was excruciatingly difficult. I felt that with each ticking moment, it was another moment closer to losing Justin. Because I was told that Justin's leukemia was a more rare form and that we were up against a clock, I felt like if we could just get to the point of transplant then he would be okay. Waiting was extra hard.

CHAPTER 10

On January 10th, Justin had his port removed and on January 11th his donor was cleared for transplant. He was scheduled to be admitted that Friday as an official BMT (bone marrow transplant) patient and begin receiving chemo and radiation. His bone marrow transplant was set for January 20th. It was our prayer answered. For going on 6 months we had the same prayer and there we were seeing God work in Justin's life. We had to find, or rather the bone marrow registry had to find, someone who was as close to a perfect match to Justin's DNA as possible. I'm his mother and I was only a half match. There was someone out there, some unknown angel, who was a nearly perfect match for Justin, 9/10. We had no idea who or where he/she was from. We just knew that someone's selflessness could give Justin a second chance. The hospital was able to tell us that it was a 30+ year old female. They told us that we could write to the donor if we wanted to. We could give our letter to the hospital, they would review it to be sure it was okay to send and didn't give any information as to who we were, and they would then send it on. I got to thinking - of course I wanted to write a letter. I also wanted to send some sort of gift. But how do you even attempt or even *begin* to try to thank someone for saving your child's life? Everything I could think of seemed entirely lacking. Justin and I both wrote a letter to the donor and we decided to buy a Pandora bracelet with an angel charm.

Some thoughts from Jessica, Justin's angel and bone marrow donor:

Wednesday November 23, 2011 (the day before Thanksgiving)- I was in Tampa, FL on my way to one of the many offices I was managing. I was near the Tampa Airport and I found a blood bank a few miles away. I drove over on my lunch break to

42

donate a pint of blood. As I entered I inquired about updating my address with the National Marrow Program. The receptionist gave me a pink piece of paper and wrote the number to the National Marrow Program for me. She told me they were not directly affiliated with the Marrow Program and I would need to contact them directly. My donation was uneventful and as I was leaving the receptionist gave me a pink angel pin, handmade, donated by a local artist for donors like myself. I decided to attach it to my rear view mirror, watching over me while I was driving, which I did quite a bit of at that time.

Thanksgiving was excellent as usual, except for the violent cold I had the following weeks. Nausea, cough, sneezing, aching, glued to my bed for over a week. My father called and insisted on bringing me some medication, my savior in so many ways. Following a brief knock on my door my father entered with a FedEx envelope and medication in his hands. He explained this envelope was on my doorstep, not sure how long it had been there. I was curious, but didn't think much of it. I eventually got around to opening it and almost fell out of my chair (or bed, not sure which). It was a packet from the National Marrow Program... about being a possible donor... about being a match... what I was wanting... what I was thinking about... what I was dreaming about... in my hand...

... I started to read through the material and my heart sank. Leukemia patient needs donor... I can do that... I couldn't read fast enough and then I saw the 800 number and called immediately. The nice lady in Minnesota told me she would mail me the consent forms I needed to fill out and return. In the mean time I needed to go to One Blood and be tested for infectious diseases. What? What kind of diseases? It made sense they would need a donor who would not transmit something bad to a leukemia patient, I get that. But... what if I have something I wasn't aware of? I looked up the local One Blood center and called for an appointment. I spoke to Fran, not just a wonderful voice on the end of the line, but my guide and mentor through this whole process. She was my gatekeeper and man did I need her, but at this point I didn't realize how much.

...Then it happened...my phone rang...out of state phone number. I stood up and walked away so I could focus on the conversation. This nice lady on the other line explained to me that I was not the first choice. There was another donor with more DNA markers in common than me but they had backed out. Backed out? I asked why someone would back out... Pregnancy, out of age range, unwilling, or unable... So they needed me to donate bone marrow by January 20th. "Why January 20th?" I asked. "Because this recipient is so sick that if they do not receive a transplant by then they will die," she said. My goodness, there was no way I was going to let that happen. I began to lose my composure and told the nice lady I was 100% committed. I thanked her for the call and walked back to my family anxiously waiting for me to speak. I looked into my mother's eyes and I didn't have to say a word. The tears were flooding my eyes and flowing down my face. "They picked me, they picked me," I said. She ran over and gave me a much needed hug as I whispered into her ear, "Merry Christmas to me." --Jessica

January 13th, Day -8. The doctors number the days so I will reference days in that way. Transplant Day is day 0. I guess that makes sense; it's a rebirth in a way for Justin. It felt like we were about to get on a roller coaster and honestly we were all scared. We knew what the doctors were telling us but in all reality we had no idea what to expect. We knew that they would be pumping Justin full of enough chemo and exposing him to enough radiation to wipe out any and all of his bone marrow. They would literally have to walk him to death's door and hope and pray that he didn't get pulled away into the ever after before they could yank him back. I kept thinking, "Does he really have cancer? Do we need to do this?" I was still in a state of denial I guess. I still couldn't believe that my son had cancer. It still made no sense to me.

January 14th, Day -7. The day started off decent enough. Justin slept fairly well the night before, thanks to Ambien, and woke up feeling okay. He finished his second round of Ara-C that morning and was on schedule to get his third round of that along with Cytoxan later that night. The morning dose of Ara-C brought with it a high fever, 103.7. Mid-morning things quickly turned. Justin became extremely nauseated. He couldn't eat or drink anything at all and slept until around 2:30 PM. I was happy when he felt okay enough to take a bath as I've seen him feel so bad before that he couldn't even consider getting out of bed. But the fever continued and per protocol, they started him on antibiotics. As the day wore on, Justin fought against a bad headache. Soon after his blood pressure started dropping. Every time the nurse came in to check it, she had him turn this way and that to try to get a better reading. It improved slightly when Justin would lie on his back but it still wasn't enough. Plus, he couldn't sleep on his back and would always roll to his side. He didn't eat anything the rest of the day and slept thanks to a cocktail of medications. I was thankful he could get enough relief to rest.

January 15th, Day -6. Justin had a rough night as he ran a high fever all night accompanied with nausea and a headache. That morning his nausea increased to the point of needing different nausea medications. Justin's fever continued and his blood pressure dropped. They decided to do a second EKG, as the first one was irregular. Chemo can cause problems with the heart. There were so many things we had to keep an eye on. Justin's entire body was being monitored in intricate detail. They ended up pausing Justin's chemo because that second EKG came back irregular as well, his blood pressure was low and he was still running a high fever. It's such a fine balance, such a thin line to walk. There is a point at which the chemo can no longer be paused and the doctors must proceed. There comes a point when things are too far gone and they would have to push through and risk losing him or stop everything and lose him for sure. How does a parent watch those events unfold? They decided to resume chemo when Justin's fever came down slightly. The doctors began talking to me about the possibility of having to move him to ICU to monitor him more closely given everything that was happening.

January 16th, Day -5. Early in the morning, or more like the middle of the night, the Rapid Response Team from ICU came in to evaluate Justin. They couldn't seem to get his blood pressure to stabilize but decided to leave him on the BMT floor and check on him frequently. Very shortly after that, they came and took Justin to ICU. I had no idea how much I would hate ICU. The nurses were experienced but there was no privacy and no possible way for Justin to rest and relax. They had a waiting room with recliners as the rooms had nothing to sit in for the parents or care givers. I wouldn't leave Justin though. They took more cultures to try to determine what was going on with Justin. They wanted to rule out illness and infection. They started giving Justin fluid and he peed it out as soon as they put it in. Then the vomiting began. Justin had always been extremely nauseated since he started chemo but the vomiting that day in ICU was ridiculous. My heart broke for him. They had him on his scheduled Zofran as well as Ativan, Phenegran and even Dexamethasone to help with nausea. Nothing seemed to ease it. His blood pressure was low, his temperature was very high, he was vomiting and he had a significant drop in his red blood cells causing him to need a transfusion. They said they may end up giving him blood pressure medicine but wanted to try something else first. His transplant wasn't delayed as the doctors said that they were going to try to "push through". They told me he would die if they just stopped everything. We had reached the point of no return. I felt completely helpless. I watched as the nurses came in busily working around each other, each with a task entirely their own. Justin lay in the fetal position in the hospital bed, the only position he could get a miniscule amount of comfort, and the nurses insisted that he lay on his back because his blood pressure dropped even lower when he rolled onto his side. He had nothing. No relief at all. They were pumping him full of poison and his entire body was screaming in argument in one form or another and Justin couldn't even find solace from rolling onto his side. I watched helpless. I had nothing I could offer him. When he was a child, I could always comfort him to a degree. There was never a time I couldn't help him at all, with anything. Now though, all I could do was watch as these people in white coats, who didn't know my son at all, worked around him. None of them tried to comfort him; they all had a job to do and did it to the best of their ability. He was vomiting into a tray and they brought in a bedside toilet for the incessant diarrhea he had as well. He had no control over his bowels and went through several pair of underwear and bedsheets. He moaned as he lay in the hospital bed and tried to find comfort. He was burning up from the fever and the vomiting just wouldn't stop. There was no rest - no relief. My heart broke wondering

45

how much his poor mind and body could take. I posted on Justin's prayers page on Facebook asking for prayers. I knew Justin needed them in any and every form possible. Later that evening the doctors spoke and decided to keep Justin in ICU overnight. His symptoms hadn't changed, although they did start him on Dopamine to try to stabilize his blood pressure. He was scheduled to be taken by ambulance to another hospital twice a day for the following 4 days for radiation. Total Body Irradiation (TBI) involves doses of radiation to the entire body to kill cancer cells and can reach places that the chemo may miss. The doctor said he would go as planned and just return to ICU after his treatment. Amidst all the difficulties, their goal was to keep him on track for transplant. With everything Justin was going through, now we would add burning the cancer cells out of his body with beams of energy to the list. What do I do as mother? What do I say? Do I tell them to stop - that they are killing my child? They would say he would die without it. What is the answer? And why don't we have more research and better methods to help these children?

You know how you say you will pray for someone or something? And you say a prayer, maybe two? Maybe you pray for that person or thing every night for a week. That's some good praying. Well, imagine for a moment that you don't stop praying. You close your eyes and you say prayers but even as you are sitting, staring at your child, you are still praying. And as you pace his bedside, you pray some more. You kneel down and touch his face and say another prayer and pretty soon you don't know when one prayer ends and another begins and then you don't know if you ever even stopped praying. Suddenly, it's all I had. Prayer was everything.

January 17th, Day -4. It was a long night in ICU. Justin was able to rest some, which was a blessing. All of his symptoms were the same except for his blood pressure which was slightly better. He was scheduled for his first round of radiation at 8:00 AM that morning. We were hopeful that he would be well enough to return to the BMT floor after. The ambulance picked us up to go over for radiation. They took Justin down the hall on a gurney and we waited for them to pull him back to the radiation room. Justin had to lie on a very uncomfortable table for 30 minutes, give or take. He couldn't move. Imagine trying to do that feeling as terrible as he felt. He vomited as we were leaving his morning radiation. The poor kid was on the gurney and I was walking beside him with his bucket when he asked to stop so he could throw up. As he finished and the paramedics pushed him on, a woman stopped me. I'd never seen her before. I didn't know her name and she didn't know mine. All she said was, "Is that your son?" I nodded yes with giant tears in my eyes and she touched my arm and said, "He's going to be okay. I know he is. I can't explain how I know. I don't even know how I know - I just know." As the tears slid out between my eyelids, I thanked her for her kind words and for stopping me to share them with me.

I'd prayed so hard and so continuously, maybe God just wanted someone to give me a message for Him. Maybe He knew I needed to hear those words of affirmation without the beeping of machines and the bustle of busy doctors and nurses. Maybe He just wanted to help my heart and mind rest for a few moments.

We returned to ICU when we got back to the hospital. A few hours later, Justin's fever broke and although still low, his blood pressure was stable and he was resting. They continued running tests on Justin and also started him on another medication as there were white blood cells in his urine. His next round of radiation was scheduled for 3:00 PM. Since his fever broke and his blood pressure was stable they let Justin go back to the BMT floor after his radiation. He would be on isolation but we were happy that he would be back on the BMT floor. Within a few hours, Justin's fever was back and his blood pressure was dropping again. I wanted to scream.

January 18th, Day -3. Justin had a great night of sleep and woke up feeling much better. He commented that he didn't remember much, if anything, about the past few days. Both rounds of radiation went well. His blood pressure was still low but his fever was back down. We were very grateful. He had an uneventful day; he just watched shows on his iPad all day. It was a welcome sight compared to how things were going just yesterday. I was so thankful! It amazed me to see the difference in a matter of hours. I would soon find out that the next few years would be a roller coaster ride of exactly this type of thing.

January 19th, Day -2. The day before transplant was a very tame day. Justin's radiation went fine and he was feeling well all day. The next day was *the* day. The plan was to have his radiation at 6:00 AM and noon and then schedule the transplant for between 6:00 PM - 7:00 PM. The following day was Day -1 and Day 0, which was fitting. It was an end and a new beginning. Everything we had done up to that point was in preparation for the next day. And we were staring it in the face. We knew that it was the day we had waited for but it was also the first step down a long road. It was scary but also exciting. Justin would be able to take a step forward towards a healthy life thanks to this transplant, thanks to his selfless donor. We felt like we had been walking in place the past 6 months, never able to go anywhere and now we were finally able to step forward with him.

I thought again of Justin's donor - of this woman, whose name we didn't even know at that time and how she would be credited for saving my son's life. I wondered about her, what she was like, if she had any kids, what she did for fun. I wondered if she could ever know what she was making possible in that hospital room. I wondered if I would ever get to meet her and hug her and thank her, or try to, for giving my son a second chance. I wondered and I wondered and I wondered...

It was interesting to me to know what she was doing in preparation for that moment.

"I had to return to One Blood to donate blood to myself. They transported my pint to the cancer center where my surgery was scheduled to occur on January 19th. On January 9th I received a phone call from the Corporate office in Minnesota and they were asking if I was still planning on donating. I couldn't understand why until I asked. They were going to pump my recipient so full of chemo that he would not survive without a transplant. I told the nice woman the only reason I wouldn't be at the cancer center on January 19th is because I had died.

The day before my surgery I was required to go to the cancer center for a final pre-operative clearance. My white blood cell count was high because I was so sick around Thanksgiving. They gave me another chest X-ray while I was there and everything was fine. I made the mistake of wearing my hair down, sitting in a waiting room full of bald cancer patients made me feel terrible. I wanted to tell them why I was there but they probably weren't as concerned about it as I was.

I arrived at the cancer center at 4am on January 19th with my dear friend. My mother was scheduled to take me but she was having stomach issues and I didn't want her anywhere near the cancer center. The intake staff was very nice and I was ready to get started. My friend waited for me and I came out of surgery around 9am. The whole procedure took about 4 hours. They extracted 6 ½ cups of marrow from my pelvis in what's called a "harvest method." There is another method less invasive but I opted for the harvest as I was told it would benefit the recipient more due to his age and his cancer. My pain level was about a 7 when I came to and I requested some pain killers which they put into my IV. I felt better within seconds. They wheeled me down to the recovery floor where I had a private room with my friend. After about 2 hours I was hungry after fasting and I wanted to get up and move around.

We left the cancer center around 1pm and headed back to my house. The first afternoon was uncomfortable but not unbearable. My mother was here to make me some dinner and make sure I had everything I needed. I spent the weekend relaxing around the house and was scheduled to return to work on Monday. I chose not to drive or exert too much energy because I was sore. I worked from home on Monday with some discomfort and returned to my office on Tuesday. By Friday I was ready to go back to the gym with minimal limitations. I couldn't believe how fast the recovery time was considering the procedure. I learned after the fact it only takes my body 2 weeks to reproduce the marrow I donated." -Jessica

January 20th, Day -1 and 0. It was transplant day. It was Justin's second day of birth. His cells were already delivered to the hospital and the doctor brought them by for us to see. It was odd really. They were in a bag, like a transfusion bag and it looked like blood. I don't know what I expected but it wasn't that. I didn't know the procedure would be so non-invasive for Justin. In good Justin form, always the jokester, he picked up the bag and pretended he was drinking the blood like in the vampire movies. They took the cells away and told us that Justin was scheduled for transplant at 7:10 PM, as it had to be 6 hours after his last radiation treatment. My parents and Jason were there also and as Justin rested, we all talked about how thankful we were for that day. Justin would wake up now and then, crack a joke and then fall back to sleep. I remember his smile so vividly. That smile of his - he still had it and it was just as bright and beautiful as ever. He laughed a lot that day. The nurses came in just after 7:00 PM to hang his cells. They checked and double checked everything they were doing. Justin slept as they had to pre-med him with Hydrocortisone, Benadryl and Tylenol. We all watched - our eyes glued to the line, as the cells made their way into Justin's body. This was it. It was happening! And then there was a clot in Justin's line and they paused his transplant. It felt like every step was torture. I felt like, if we could just get past this part we could handle anything. After a little while, they finally got the cells going again and Justin was on his way to his second chance. The moment we waited for so long was upon us and as we breathed out a sigh of relief, we took in the unknown.

January 21st, Day +1. The following day was day +1 - imagine it. Imagine that your days are numbered and then just like that, you get to start over. It wouldn't be easy; we knew it would be hell but we also knew what the alternative would be. They monitored Justin longer than usual after his transplant because his blood pressure spiked and his heart rate dropped. They started him on TPN (Total Parenteral Nutrition) and lipids because he hadn't eaten in over a week. He was on Marinol (the pill form of marijuana) as they were hoping it would help with nausea and increase his appetite, which it did. Jason had to leave on Day +1 so I drove him to the airport while my parents stayed with Justin. Pretty soon it would be only Justin and me again.

The heavy doses of chemo and radiation carried a substantial price that we would soon watch unfold. By day +2, Justin developed terrible Mucositis and was in a great deal of pain. Mucositis can occur anywhere in the digestive tract, from the mouth to the anus. Justin had it in his mouth, his throat and further down in his digestive tract. The tissue along his digestive tract was sloughing off and being expelled through his stool. They put him on a PCA pump to administer morphine for the pain. Watching Justin experience the things he did was like watching him come apart - come unraveled. I had a front row seat to the devastating effects that cancer, chemo and radiation would have on my son and it broke my heart every single day. Again, I felt helpless. That feeling would be one I would get quite acquainted with, yet never be okay with. The mucositis continued to worsen over the next couple of days. They increased Justin's morphine to try to combat the pain. He got up and walked around on Day +3, but on Day +4 he couldn't get out of bed. His platelets were at 13k (normal platelets are 150k – 450k) so he was given a transfusion. On Day +5, Justin's mouth pain was worse but everything else was about the same. His counts continued to drop, which was expected. I knew they would drop drastically as they had been but I wouldn't feel any kind of peace until they started to go back up. Isn't that how it goes? At first, all I wanted was for him to get the transplant and then I was focused on those counts going back up. Maybe that was the way of it though. If we thought about it all at once, we wouldn't be able to do any of it. Maybe we had to take it piece by piece, moment by moment and deal with what was right in front of us. Maybe that was the key to making it through. We tried to pass the time by playing games and watching movies.

To make matters worse, Justin's PICC site in his arm was a mess. He ended up with a chemical burn from the bio patch the nurses used. It seemed as though everything on and in Justin's body was struggling. Day +7 was Justin's worst day since transplant. He was in a great deal of pain from the side effects. They increased his morphine to try to help him feel better, but before I knew it he was shaking and throwing up. I asked for nausea meds for him, he got them and he threw up again. He continued to have diarrhea. Finally, I asked them to back off on the morphine as I was worried it was contributing to his nausea. We finally got him settled down and he started running a fever. They started him on three different antibiotics and ran blood cultures to check for an infection. They ended up taking him off morphine by the end of the day and putting him on a different pain med called Dilaudid as they hoped it wouldn't cause as much itching and nausea. His mucositis was so bad he couldn't swallow. He used a suction straw to suck the spit out of his mouth. I looked at him and wondered if there was a single part of his poor tattered body that wasn't in pain from the transplant and all that came with it.

Just after midnight, on Day +8, Justin almost had to be moved to ICU as his blood pressure dropped. He was having odd foot pain and pressure and severe mouth pain and was given another dose of Lidocaine, some Tylenol to drop his fever, his antibiotics and Dilaudid. The next thing I knew Justin was asking me to crunch up Oreo's in ice cream as he sat up in bed and watched TV. What a sight to see! I can't put into words what that did for my heart. We were definitely on a roller coaster and we rode out that high as long as we could.

Justin and I were up most of the night since he slept most of the day before. He got a blood transfusion around 2:00 PM and was scheduled to get a platelet transfusion later that night. He was still in a battle with his nausea. He seemed to have had a short reprieve in the middle of the night but it came back in full force. Justin had nausea for going on 8 months at that point. It was constant and completely miserable. The fetal position was his favorite position. It was where he found the most relief, and even then it wasn't much. He was on every nausea cocktail you could imagine and nothing helped. The Marinol at least allowed him to eat. That didn't mean he would keep it down. One day after multiple times vomiting I told him, "I promise you son that there will come a day when you won't be nauseated all the time." I believed it when I said it to him. However, there did come a time when I regretted saying that at all.

I left the hospital for a little bit that day to go to the apartment and check the mail. I hated leaving Justin and I only did it when necessary but when I stepped outside I felt like life was breathed into me. It's amazing what fresh air can do. I so badly wished Justin could be out there, even for just a few minutes. I knew what a difference it could make for him.

Day +10. The chemo and radiation killed all of Justin's bone marrow. The bone marrow is where your red and white blood cells and platelets are made. Your cells are where your DNA comes from. Justin had no bone marrow and no cells and then he had this new, healthy bone marrow transplanted. Literally every cell in Justin's body was changing. Often throughout Justin's illness, I found myself wondering what he must feel like. I wondered how the chemo and radiation made him feel. I knew what it was like to be sick and to not feel well but I just could not imagine what it felt like to have poison pumped into your body. I couldn't wrap my head around it. Likewise, I couldn't imagine what it must have been like to have every single cell in your body change. I thought about what that must have been like for Justin, not only on a physical level but also on a mental one. He was changing, his very being was changing. What would that mean for him? And who would he be after that transformation? Because we all say all day long that cancer doesn't change you, that it can't take real things from you, but that's bullshit. It can. That day he made the comment, "I feel like I can feel every cell in my body." I couldn't imagine what he must have been experiencing. Knowing what the process entailed and understanding how Justin's body was changing entirely from the inside out made me wish for the thousandth time that I could take his place. He was having some light sensitivity, feet and leg pain and his Mucositis was still awful.

January 31st, Day +11. The day didn't bring any relief. It was a tough day. The day before Justin had moments of reprieve but that January 31st was a really hard day. He was still on a lot of medications for nausea and was trying to sleep a lot. His feet were hurting and his skin was becoming particularly sensitive to every touch. I'm a hugger. I always hug on Justin and touch him and now it was hurting him. It was getting to where all I could do was look at him lying there in that hospital bed and pray to God for relief for him. I was doing that anyway but now I couldn't even touch him to give him comfort. His hair had fallen out before, grew back and started falling out again and his PICC line was horribly sore. His Mucositis had gotten so bad that they decided to not give him Day +11 of

Methotrexate, a drug used to prevent the cancer from spreading to the central nervous system. I couldn't wait for that damn transplant and only 11 days post and I was wondering if it was the right way to go. Justin seemed to be coming apart at the seams.

February 1st, Day +12. We made it to another month. We were out of January and into February. I had increased hope with each passing day so to make it to a new month was encouraging. I was thankful for every single moment in every single day with Justin. That day started off a little better as Justin was actually awake and coherent. We watched *The Sandlot*. The doctors increased his pain meds as the pain in his feet was excruciating and his mucositis was worsening by the day. They actually put lidocaine patches on his feet to help alleviate the pain. They were beginning to think that one of the chemos, Vincristine, was the culprit of his feet pain. They increased his Marinol as well in hopes that it would help decrease his nausea. He did get both a platelet and a blood transfusion that day. That was expected. His counts were still bottomed out. Justin was on the worst kind of see-saw. His days were up and down. He would have parts of a decent day and the next day would be terrible. He continued to struggle with vomiting and diarrhea.

February 4th, Day +15. Before I even start on my rant, let me say this: Please pay attention to everything that everyone does who has contact with your child! That is one of the reasons I never left Justin, except for 30 minutes to an hour and only when nothing was supposed to be going on with him. Doctors and nurses are not perfect. Don't get me wrong, I'm very appreciative of everything they did for my son but I also know they are human. From the time of diagnosis, I started learning. I looked things up online, I read books and I asked questions - all so I could be an active part in Justin's care. I wasn't that person who sat back while things happened to and with my son. I was standing right beside him, watching everything. I knew what meds he took and the dosages. Things changed obviously and sometimes it took me a bit to adjust to new times, meds, dosages and procedures but I did. The doctors changed one of Justin's anti-rejection drugs, Tacrolimus, from IV form to oral. They did that because of the pain in his legs and feet. Their hope was that the oral medication wouldn't cause him so much pain. They still weren't positive what caused his leg and foot pain but were concerned it was the Tacrolimus or the chemo, Vincristine, they had given him prior to transplant. They stressed how important it was for him to take the medication on time, every day, twice a day. The nurse brought in his morning dose 45 minutes late and handed it to him after waking him up. He took it and within 30 minutes he threw up. Because he had been having so much nausea, I didn't think too much of it. A couple of hours later my mom noticed a syringe with something still in it on the counter. I knew that nothing should be over there so I jumped up to see what it was. It said, "Tacrolimus." I was immediately confused because she

52

had given the Tac to him hours before. I took it out into the hall to ask the first nurse I saw about it. I asked to her to look up his meds to see if he was supposed to have 2 syringes of Tac. Then I went back in the room and found the tag for the liquid he took orally. I didn't recognize the drug name but what greatly concerned me was that it said it was supposed to be given through an IV. I was extremely upset! I found the charge nurse, told her what happened and she wrote it up. She said that it was probably what made him throw up. The drug she gave him orally that was supposed to be given IV was actually Lasix, a drug to make him pee. His Tacrolimus was very late by that time because of everything and I was pissed off. Aside from the mix up with his meds, Justin had a decent afternoon and was even able to watch a movie. His counts had stayed the same. That's one thing I got in the habit of – always checking his labs. It was odd because I would wake up early specifically to go get a print out his counts. I learned how to read them. I learned what was important for him and I studied his labs with a mixture of hope and concern.

February 5th, Day +16. Justin's WBC (white blood count) wasn't moving. It should have been increasing by then. He should have been producing some white blood cells. The doctors said that they may want to give him a medication to help with that. It would stimulate his white blood cells and help them increase. I'm clueless as to the healthcare field. I have been blown away at all of the procedures and medications that can aid in just about any area of need. I read that only 4% of federal funding is solely dedicated to childhood cancer research. That just doesn't make sense to me. I understand that more adults get cancer than kids, but I also understand that where adults lose an average of 15 years of life to cancer, kids lose an average of 71 years. I certainly don't want to ignore the adults who have cancer or take away from them. Hell, my mother had breast cancer. I simply want the funding for childhood cancer to make some sense. And it just doesn't.

Justin received a platelet transfusion as well as a blood transfusion as his red blood was at 8k, which was the lowest it could go before a transfusion was needed. I was grateful for the blood and platelet transfusions but they didn't come without risk - fever, chills, shortness of breath, back pain, itching, dizziness and the list goes on. Justin's PICC site was about the same. The actual site looked a little better but he still had torn skin all around the area. His skin was incredibly sensitive. His nausea was still terrible.

February 6th, Day +17. There are things that have happened to Justin that the doctors warned us about, side effects that they said could happen but probably wouldn't. Of course, the "probably wouldn't" certainly did with Justin. And then there were things that happened to Justin that no one saw coming at all. There was no preparation for those things because Justin was a first for many of them.

Justin woke up with a fever. He was in and out of sleep but conveyed to me that his jaw hurt. Minutes after telling me, a doctor came in and I told him what Justin said. He looked inside Justin's mouth but said he didn't see anything, rattled off why it might hurt and briskly left the room. Justin was miserable, I could tell. I asked him if I could look. I asked him to pick up and move his tongue and then I saw the issue. His gums were swollen on the left, bottom side and had nearly covered all of his teeth. I called for the doctor to come back in. He looked again and was visibly shaken. He ordered a CAT scan of his head and a chest X-ray. In addition, he prescribed different antibiotics. He worried there was an infection causing his gums to swell and we both knew that an infection was bad news for Justin. He still didn't have the white blood cells to fight anything. My heart dropped into my stomach and I immediately got on the Prayers for Justin page on Facebook pleading for prayers for his latest issue. His labs indicated a drop in red blood (6.6 then) so he received another transfusion. They also ordered the Neupogen shots to try to give his white blood cells a boost. Justin was a mess. There were so many things happening all at once. Justin's fever was rising significantly, he had thrown up all day, his legs and arms were peeling from the radiation he received before the transplant and he was still in a great deal of jaw pain. He didn't want to push the PCA button for his pain in fear that it would just increase his nausea. Again, that question of choosing between bad and worse. What helps one thing could hurt another. He was in agony. And all I could do was sit beside him, hold his hand and watch him suffer. Watching your child suffer, knowing there is nothing you can do is an entirely different kind of agony.

February 7th, Day +18. How does he do it? Nighttime comes but it doesn't bring relief for him and when the sun rises, his pain is still there. There was no reprieve for him. It's just more - more pain, more nausea, more issues for him to combat. It wasn't the first time I'd asked but I wondered how much more he could take. Justin was still in a tremendous amount of pain because of his jaw/mouth/neck. He continued to run a fever but the nausea eased off. He finally started pushing his PCA button in the middle of the night but we couldn't seem to get his pain under control. His mouth, gums and neck were swollen. I put an ice pack on his jaw as we waited for an ENT (ears, nose and throat) doctor to come look at his mouth. The doctors were talking about taking an aspirate of his gums to send off for testing. Naturally, they put him back on isolation. The doctors increased his pain meds and they finally started to have an effect on him. He was so drugged that he was in and out of sleep. In his moments of consciousness, he tried to text friends. I had no idea what in the world he was saying to them because he was entirely out of it. At one point, when he dozed off again, I reached to take his phone from him and put it away. As I reached for it he snatched my arm and said, "So…we meet again." I busted out laughing and he just smiled. I have never stopped being amazed at his sense of humor through everything. The way he was able to still smile and find humor baffled me. Granted, this time he was drugged up but nonetheless.

Soon after, the infectious disease doctors came in to look at Justin's mouth. They said they were *very* concerned. They thought he had one of two infections that I couldn't begin to tell you the names of because I couldn't pronounce them to know how to spell them. They decided to put him on a different antibiotic, Meropenum, that they keep in reserve for severe infections. I'm sure you have heard that if you take an antibiotic for too long you can become immune to it. So, news to me, there are some antibiotics that are never used for that very purpose. The idea is that having zero exposure to an antibiotic should make it more effective in treating certain illnesses. After talking with the doctor, I had a breakdown. He told me that they didn't know if that antibiotic would work but it was the only thing they could try. He said if it didn't work, Justin could die. They just didn't have any other options. Again, I don't know how someone processes information like that. All I knew to do was pray and ask others to pray with me. I paced. I cried. And I prayed. And at times, I would just stop and look at him and rub his head and love him. Somewhere deep inside my heart and gut I knew that he had to be okay. It wasn't a question for me. But trying to convince my mind of that was another story. My mind liked to have unspeakable thoughts that if I even gave a voice to would break me. My mind played through every single scenario. I don't know why, maybe in preparation for what could happen. But honestly, it wouldn't matter how many times I played the worst possible outcome in my head, nothing would ever prepare me for it.

The doctors were concerned about the swelling because if it got too much worse, it could interfere with his breathing. They were still planning on having an oral surgeon come aspirate his gums and send it off for testing in addition to having an ENT doctor come and look at the back of his throat with a camera. There were just so many issues for this kid to have to deal with. There were still so many problems I didn't understand and I still had countless questions as I lay down to try to sleep that night.

You know that feeling of complete comfort you get when you find that perfect position when going to sleep? It doesn't happen very often but it's this "Sweet Spot" that you occasionally come across and once you find it, you don't want to move, not an inch, because you know you won't be able to find it again? Well, as I lay down to go to sleep that night, I noticed it, and not only did I notice it but it was the best "Sweet Spot" I'd ever found. It was ultimate comfort and I noticed that even when I moved, it was still there. Then I realized that it was God's embrace - his comfort surrounding me, all the prayers reaching around us and holding us. I can't speak for Justin but I'd say he felt it too. He rested well that night.

February 8th, Day +19. Justin's blood cultures came back showing that there were bacteria growing in his bloodstream. The doctors added another antibiotic, making a total of three. They said that the bacteria that was growing was resistant but the Meropenem was very strong. The doctors weren't even allowed to prescribe it unless they got permission from the infectious disease doctors, which they did. They said it's like pulling out a bazooka when you were using a shotgun before. In addition to everything else, because somehow there just wasn't enough wrong, there was some concern with Justin's kidneys as they were showing elevated levels of creatinine. "Creatinine is a chemical waste molecule that is generated from muscle metabolism. It is transported through the bloodstream to the kidneys where it is filtered out and disposed of in the urine. If the kidneys become impaired, the creatinine levels in the blood will rise due to poor clearance."[5] It was a long few days but Justin somehow managed to smile and make jokes along the way. Somehow amidst everything that was happening, it was Justin keeping it all together. He didn't see me struggle. I would leave the room to cry. My shower time every day was my "break down and cry" time. I just let go and let it out. Crying in the shower was very therapeutic. The water washed my tears away and after 15 minutes of a combination of crying and praying, I was ready to face the next little while of whatever came our way. I didn't want Justin to see me break down because I didn't want him to worry about me. That was Justin's way. He would be more worried about me and how I was dealing with things than about himself and I knew he needed to focus on just getting better.

February 9th, Day +20. The day brought some good news: the antibiotics were working. Justin's pain had eased and the swelling in his gums came down slightly. It was still red and angry looking but overall he felt better. His nausea was still rather intense which just made him feel miserable. His fever came down but kept trying to go back up. He couldn't walk more than just a few feet due to how weak he was as well as his neuropathy. Neuropathy caused part of his feet to hurt and tingle and he lost feeling in large sections of his feet and toes. We were ecstatic that his ANC (Absolute Neutrophil Count) was up to 760. "A normal ANC falls between 1,500 and 8,000. The most important white blood cell in fighting infection is the neutrophil. When a patient's ANC falls below 1000 the patient is considered to be neutropenic, meaning that they are at a much higher risk for infection."[6] Justin's ANC was finally climbing. We knew that God was answering our prayers. We knew that He heard us and that with so many people coming together to pray for Justin, how couldn't He take care of him?

February 11th, Day +22. Justin was taken off isolation the day before but was put back on it that morning. They were testing for some viruses. His nausea and vomiting continued to persist, making him feel terrible. He was throwing up 4-5 times a day. They sent off a chimerism test (a test that would show if Justin was all donor cells or if he had any of his original cells) that would tell us if the transplant was successful but we hadn't heard back about it yet. Later that day the doctor came in to talk to us and told us that less than 5% of patients have the problems that Justin has had. I thought back about it. The doctors would talk to us about things that Justin would have to undergo and they would tell us all of the possible side effects and then add on, as if to give us some relief, that most of the really bad side effects only happen in less than 5% of patients. Justin had quickly become the "less than 5%." He not only fell into that category with every treatment, medicine and procedure but he started a new category with issues he developed that no one had before. I knew that Justin was extraordinary but good grief! Justin received other treatments and instead of finding relief when the doctors would tell us how rare some side effects were, we felt terror because we knew that Justin would experience the whole gambit.

February 14th, Day +25. From today's report: "No evidence of male host cells...a pattern consistent with (XX) female donor cells in all 500 interphase cells examined." In other words, the transplant had been completely successful up to that point. He was showing only his donor cells and none of his own. They would continue to check as his counts grew and that could change but the news was amazing! With everything Justin was going through, we were beside ourselves with relief. And while that news was amazing, there were still many tests that they had to do to be sure things were on track. Justin was scheduled to have a bone marrow biopsy on that Friday to confirm the report we received, that his donor cells are growing rather than his own. They would have to continue to test this for many years after transplant. In addition, we heard that we were going to get to leave the hospital on Monday or Tuesday of that next week. We were praying that the doctors could get his neuropathy figured out and manipulate some of his medications that would allow us to leave. We knew we would have to stay in Houston until late April and come into the outpatient clinic at least 3 times a week for checkups and transfusions but I felt like it would do Justin a world of good to just get out of the hospital. There were still so many things that he was up against but we definitely welcomed any bit of good news. On top of all that, Justin was getting some relief from his nausea. I asked the doctors about starting Justin on Emend but they didn't think it would work at that point because Emend was more for chemo induced nausea and they felt that Justin had moved beyond that. I'd heard so much about it though and I just wanted them to try it because they had literally tried everything else and nothing was working. Justin was miserable all the time because he was so nauseated and lately it was much worse. The doctor finally decided to try Emend and it helped greatly. I didn't know if it always would. I didn't know how long the relief would last but I knew Justin finally stopped throwing up and his nausea greatly diminished and for that I was thankful. I was thankful for those moments when Justin could rest, nausea free.

February 17th, Day +28. When you go from complete misery and just wanting to sleep until the pain and nausea pass to working out in your hospital room, you know God is working overtime to answer the many prayers that so many people had offered up. Justin started working out and going on walks. He felt much better! He had a bone marrow biopsy and aspirate as well as a spinal tap to see the progress he was making. The doctors thought he had thrush on top of his long list of ailments. His tongue was thick with a white coating. That seemed okay and deal-withable to me. I knew it was one more thing but my gosh at what he had been through! I think I would take thrush over just about anything he'd had any day. Not that it worked that way. It's not like if he got one thing, he wouldn't get another. It's not like we could actually breathe any kind of sigh of relief at something as miniscule as thrush. But right then, given everything, it's all we could do. We learned to just appreciate a moment when Justin didn't want to throw up or wasn't in a tremendous amount of pain. It's funny how we took all of those many moments for granted before he got sick and then we found ourselves begging, praying and pleading for them. Perspective.

"Justin has always been team first...he's never me first. Justin was always the kid that never complained about any position Coach put him in, whether that be sitting the bench, trying out 3rd or starting 2nd base. He always worked as hard as he could and put his head down, always moved forward and it paid off in the end when he started 2nd base for the state championship game. He got his chance because of his attitude and perseverance and work ethic and we won a ring with him." – Dominic Moreno, Friend & Teammate

Day +32, February 21st. Justin brought a lot to his fight with cancer. He came in strong in mind and body. He was a very determined, driven young man. He wasn't afraid of hard work. It's true that he had no idea what lay in store for him but what is also true is that Justin was all heart. There wasn't anything he couldn't do. Not only would he push through but he often did so with a smile. And that is what led to day +32 when Justin and I packed up room 48 and walked out of the BMT floor with Justin happy and feeling strong. It was the first time in 40 days that Justin had left the BMT floor.

As far as we knew, Justin was on the road to recovery. As far as we knew, the worst was behind us. As far as we knew, we made it, *he* made it. But, we would come to find out that we didn't really know anything at all.

CHAPTER 11

Justin had never been to the apartment even though I'd had it for over a month by the time he was released from the hospital. He was incredibly happy when I got him in and settled. He loved that we had privacy after living in the Ronald McDonald House for 5 months. We shared a room that had twin beds and a bedside table between them. After sleeping in the hospital for 40 nights, we felt like we were in a presidential suite of some sort. We seemed to acclimate to anything we had. We went from sleeping at home to sleeping in a hospital room, to sleeping in a room at the Ronald McDonald House to sleeping in an ICU hospital room (which isn't even sleeping) to sleeping in the amazing beds at the apartment. We also had a living room with a couch that pulled out into a bed and a full kitchen. We were on the second floor and Justin always needed help walking anymore, especially walking up the steps to the second floor. We looked at it as a way to build strength for him.

I found myself doing things that I hadn't done before. I wasn't use to carrying the brunt of everything. However, throughout the process of Justin's treatments, I found myself doing more and more until one day I was doing everything. That was okay. It was hard and I went to bed exhausted most nights but I was fulfilled in ways I had never been before. And everything I was doing was teaching me so much about myself and was preparing me for what was to come. Those steps weren't only building Justin's strength, they were building my strength as well.

We did some normal things for a while when Justin was out of the hospital. I actually went grocery shopping and Justin and I both made dinner. He did school work on the days he felt up to it. He was still on track to graduate in May so on his "good" days he would plug away at his school work all day long, from dawn to dusk. He was still very weak and was often nauseated so we didn't go out much at all, except to go to the hospital several times a week for his appointments. He had his counts checked to be sure that everything was moving in the right direction. Jenna came out to see Justin again. We were both always thankful for her visits. She had a way of making us both laugh and lifting Justin up. It was hard on Jordan to not be able to get away from work to come visit more but we understood that he had a family to take care of.

One of the biggest battles was continuing to keep Justin's mental and emotional side up. In order for him to be in the best shape to fight the physical toll that the treatment took on him, he needed to be mentally and emotionally strong. It was still my mission to keep his mind busy all the time. I took him to hockey, baseball and football games. We went to movies, he played video games and we watched TV. When people came to visit, it always perked him up. Justin was in and out of the hospital with fevers here and there. We always had our bags packed ready to go. He hated it - going to the hospital at all hours of the night and day, being hooked up to several different lines, never sleeping, always having doctors and nurses come in. He knew the routine by then and he hated it, but he did it.

It was baseball season and as Justin was fighting to be well so he could go home, his high school baseball team was knee deep in another great season. His buddy, Shane Woodson, sent me a very poignant picture of Justin's jersey hanging in the dugout. He explained that the team took the jersey with them and hung it up in the dugout at every game. That is what drove Justin - the way his team kept him close. It inspired to him to fight harder to leave Houston. Many, many amazing people from all over the world, often people we hadn't met before, sent Justin mail. It was wonderful to see and one of the things Justin most looked forward to. He loved interaction with the outside world and to know he was being thought of and prayed for by so many. Ryan Brewer from Albuquerque, New Mexico often arranged for us to go watch the Astros play baseball. Ryan played minor league ball and knew many of the coaches and players. He knew of Justin's love for baseball. He knew that it lifted Justin up to be able to go watch those games. Watching baseball was bittersweet for Justin. He loved the sport; actually he was flat passionate about it. It ran in his veins. Watching those games breathed life into him. But it did something else too. It reminded Justin of something he couldn't do anymore. Not only could he not do it now but he wasn't sure if he would ever be able to play ball again. He watched with such a longing in his eyes, a yearning for a life that seemed so long ago.

"As I got to know the Solomons and became really good friends with Jennifer, I made a promise to Jenn that I was in this to help for the long haul. Anything they needed that I could help with, I was all in. I really didn't know why I was in this for a family that I saw maybe 3 or 4 times a year...there was something about them and the situation I felt

I needed to help with." –Ryan Brewer

Baseball was life to Justin for so long, ever since he was a little boy and started T-Ball at age 4. All he ever wanted to do was play baseball for as long as he could. We thought for sure that would be at least college. We still had hope.

"I will always be impressed with how much he loved baseball and how hard he worked to impress the coach, make the team, and become a starter. It makes me cry as I recall how much he has suffered since, but I am always impressed how he has hung in there and progressed to where he is now. He is a remarkable young man whom the Lord has selected to be an example to us all." –Larry Welsh (Justin's Papa)

In mid-March, Justin started physical therapy. We were at the hospital nearly every single day between Justin's outpatient visits and his PT. Justin's physical therapist was wonderful. She and Justin became fast friends and Justin worked very, very hard during his sessions. Justin really noticed his neuropathy and that he had foot drop. "Foot drop stems from weakness or paralysis of the muscles that lift the foot. It's the inability to lift the front part of the foot."[7] We knew the chemo drugs were responsible for that as well. It wasn't going to be easy but Justin worked diligently every day to help his body recover from the blow it had taken.

By the end of March 2012, we were back at the Ronald McDonald House in Houston as we could only stay in the apartment for 3 months. It's hard to go backwards but as always we adjusted. One day I got a phone call from Deon Brown. He asked me if we would be able to fly home to Farmington for Knothole Day if he could get it arranged. Knothole Day represents the opening of baseball season in Farmington. Farmington Amateur Baseball Congress has opening ceremonies, following which the two rival high schools battle it out on the field. It would be a great day to make it home but I had no idea how I would make that happen. Justin was in the hospital regularly for outpatient meds and treatments. He was still wearing his HEPA-filter mask (an air cleaner that can catch and destroy any virus, bacteria or mold spores quickly) most of the time and I had no idea how his doctor would allow him to go. Not to mention the fact that airplanes were a big no-no for him. There were far too many germs and it was all circulated air. He had to be in the hospital that Friday before and the Monday after but I decided to look into it. I didn't say anything to Justin right away because I didn't want him to be disappointed if he couldn't go. I emailed his doctor and she actually said it was fine if we could make it a day trip. I figured it wasn't going to work out because there was no way we could make it a day trip. I called Deon to tell him the news and he just wasn't having it. He said, "What if we could get a private plane to pick you guys up, bring you to Farmington for the ceremonies and then take you back to Houston that night? Could you do it then?" I was in shock. I had no experience with private planes but he said he knew someone. He called me back later that day and said it was done. He then sent me the itinerary and said he would see us on Saturday, April 21st. I couldn't believe it; it looked like Justin was going to get to go home for the first time since he left Farmington 8 months prior. I knew that was going to mean the world to him. When I told Justin he just stared at me speechless. He couldn't believe he was going home but even more so he couldn't believe that people went to so much effort to get him there. We were both moved and tremendously happy. I spoke about things that kept Justin "up" mentally and this was gigantic on that list!!! We agreed to not tell anyone in Farmington, except for Justin's dad, that we were coming.

CHAPTER 12

Sometimes there are moments that are perfect, moments where you wouldn't change a single thing and they contain so much happiness that they remain with you forever. And sometimes, if you're really, really lucky, you have an entire day like that.

We loaded the car, left early and drove to the small airport in Houston to catch our plane. Neither Justin nor I had ever been in a private plane so we weren't quite sure what to expect. We waited in the lobby with just a couple of things: Justin's bag of medication and our sweatshirts. It was just a day trip so we figured we didn't need much. The plane was obviously very small, amazing and small. Justin was nauseated in flight. He threw up a couple of times before we landed in Farmington and tried to sleep the rest of the time so he wouldn't have to worry with that terrible, nausea feeling. For Justin, the anticipation of being home, seeing his dog, being with his friends and watching baseball was worth all of the nausea. We landed in Farmington and Brandy Brown, Deon's wife, was there to pick us up. She had everything that Justin could possibly want or need including a cooler with drinks and fruit. Justin was getting five-star treatment. She took us to Justin's dad's house where, for the very first time, Justin met his dog Apollo. Apollo is an expensive Alaskan malamute that Justin begged me to buy him months before he became ill. There was no way I could afford a purebred dog like Apollo, so I told Justin no. After becoming sick, some of Justin's friends got together and collected money from the community at the Connie Mack World Series to buy Justin that dog he wanted so much. It was heart-warming. They couldn't get the puppy until that following December when we were already in Houston, so Justin had never met Apollo. Oh my goodness the way Apollo looked at him. Their eyes locked and it was like Apollo knew that he was Justin's. The instant love between the two of them was a site to behold. We went into Jason's house where Jason showed Justin a proclamation from the mayor of Farmington, stating that April 21st, 2012 was officially Justin Solomon Day. The way that the community came together for this kid set my heart on fire. It was beautiful to see. Justin felt loved and incredibly special. Still, no one knew that Justin was in town. I couldn't wait to see the reaction of his friends and his baseball buddies when he walked out onto the field at Rickett's Park.

We got onto the business at hand. Justin and I climbed into Brandy's truck to head towards the ballpark and Jason went to pick up Justin's jersey. We were in total stealth mode to not give away that Justin was there so we parked on a hill behind the ballfields and waited for Jason to arrive with Justin's jersey. From the truck, we watched as teams were lining up to make their way onto the field. We knew that Justin wouldn't get in without at least a few people seeing him but that was okay. Jason showed up with his jersey and he changed in the truck. Brandy drove the truck to the bottom of the hill and we waited there for just the right time. The plan was for the MC to begin talking about Justin, how he'd been doing since transplant and how much he was missed that day. Then he would say something about there being a special guest and he would begin playing Justin's baseball walk-up song, "Rock Star" by R. Kelly. When that song started playing, Justin would walk onto the field where his friends would already be. The anticipation of that moment was building by the second. Justin couldn't stop smiling. That was the stuff that fueled his fight. Moments like those were what he would depend on in his toughest moments.

Brandy and Deon thought of everything. They even had a chair made for him, with his name and number on the back, because they knew he wouldn't be able to stand for long periods of time. We had the chair in hand and Jason and I were ready to walk with our son onto the field. We could hear muffled talking but we weren't sure what was being said. Then we heard the song we had heard so many times as his walk-up song. That alone made the blood course faster through our veins. We followed Justin as he walked through the gate, between the bleachers, through the field gate and onto the field. We watched as the crowd exploded out of their seats upon seeing him and as his entire team rushed him, scooping him up in their arms, taking turns hugging him. I just stood there, stood back and watched as love took a tangible form. I was overcome with gratitude. The crowd was still cheering as Justin's best friend, Brady Colebrook, gave me a, "Why the heck didn't you tell me?!?!" look. And I just smiled. As I said before, there are moments in this life that are perfect, moments that fill you from head to toe, moments that you will remember in such vivid detail for all of time. That day was a series of those moments. It was a sight to witness; Justin's friends gathered around him with the community looking on with smiles on their faces and their hearts full of well wishes. I was thankful for so many things in that moment: for my son's health, for his amazing friends and for a community who stood behind him.

After the hugs and welcome from his teammates, Justin walked to home plate, took the mic and said a few words. He expressed his heartfelt gratitude to everyone for their outpouring of love and support for him. I was so proud of him. He had been through hell but there he was smiling, happy and overflowing with gratitude.

We only had a few hours there before we had to fly back and Justin packed those hours with love and laughter. He sat in the dugout as his high school, Piedra Vista, played their rival, Farmington High, and cheered his team on. He mingled with old friends in the stands and met new ones. He posed while I took what probably felt like thousands of pictures. And then he had to say his goodbyes. He hugged everyone a little tighter, with the comforting thought the he would be back home for good in about a month. He knew he could ride out a high like that until he was able to go home. Things seemed brighter as we made our way back to Brandy's truck and drove back to the airport to catch our plane. Hope was in the air and it was palpable.

CHAPTER 13

Many things in life build up to other moments. They are stepping stones and prepare us for what's next in our lives. Justin and I had been in Houston for 8 months, only going home once. After many outpatient visits and several inpatient hospital stays, Justin was finally cleared to go home. We were ecstatic. We packed the car barely making everything fit with the seats in the back down. I left plenty of room for Justin to recline his chair since he continued to struggle with extreme bouts of nausea and I knew he would need to lie back and get in the fetal position to find some comfort. We had a 17 hour drive staring us in the face but we were more than ready to go. Neither of us cared if we ever saw Houston again. The medical care was top notch, nothing short of amazing. However, that city would forever more be a city of pain for us. We were happy to be leaving it behind. Our plan was to make it to Amarillo the first night and on into Farmington the next day.

After a couple of long days of driving, we made it home. Justin was deeply happy to be back. He did a lot of "normal" things. He hung out with his friends and went to the high school while the boys had baseball practice. There were some days he didn't do anything. He was just too miserable with his nausea and fatigue to muster the strength to leave the house. Not to mention, he had to be careful being in crowds because his immune system was incredibly compromised. It definitely took some getting used to. Justin continued on in his school work and was on track to graduate with his class. We were grateful as those boys meant so much to him and walking with them at graduation was deeply significant to him. It looked like the boys were going to the state championship for baseball so he, of course, planned on going to support them as they had supported him for the past year.

Justin rode down to Albuquerque with his team on the bus and his father and I followed. He warmed up some with the team and met up with them for their batting practice. He was right there, never missing a beat. He stayed in the hotel room with us at night as he was still extremely nauseated and still often vomited. But he woke up early and bounced out of the hotel room to go cheer on his team and his friends. Regardless of the nausea, he felt good. He was happy. And on May 13th, Piedra Vista High School won the state championship for the 3rd year in a row. The boys were thrilled and Justin was glad he was there and could be a part of something so special.

Justin was diagnosed with cancer the summer before he was to be a senior in high school. What a crappy time to become ill, as if there is ever a good time to be told you have cancer. There were plenty rites of passage that Justin missed out on. On top of that, we wondered over the 8 months spent in Houston if Justin was going to be able to get his work completed so he could graduate and walk with his class. That kid busted his butt on his decent days to stay on track. He was surprisingly responsible for someone in his position. He felt like hell most days and certainly had an understandable excuse if he didn't graduate on time. No one would have faulted him. But he pushed and dug in and he did it! On May 23rd, Justin was lined up to walk with his very best friend, Brady. I was on overlove, overdrive, overproud, overthankful, overhappy, etc. Things came together in such a way that I stood back and just thanked God. All the pain, all the tears, all the medications and the nausea and the worry and the helplessness led us to that beautiful day; the day when Justin would graduate high school after battling for his life. I got word that Justin was nauseated in line as he was waiting to walk. Jason ran out to the car and got his nausea meds which I then handed off to him as he walked by us on his way to his seat on the field. The fact that Justin could even stay upright and walk at graduation was a success in itself. We asked if he wanted a wheelchair but he refused. This was something he needed to do. Yes, we were still juggling and adjusting and finagling this new way of life but we were making it work. When they called Justin's name, the crowd clapped loudly as he accepted his diploma and gave all glory to God. That day will always stand out in my mind and heart. It showed everyone that even at your worst, even when you're in the most pain you've ever experienced, even when your body is broken, you can push through with your mind and heart and do remarkable things.

As per tradition with most people graduating from high school, Justin's friends had a big trip planned after graduation to Mexico. Unfortunately, Justin couldn't go. His immune system was just too suppressed and Mexico was absolutely no place for a kid who recently received a bone marrow transplant, so we planned something else. It wasn't as grand as going to another country with all of your closest friends. We chose to take him to

Florida. We decided on Disney, Islands of Adventure and the beach, of course. We got permission from his BMT doctor to take him. It was only months before that he had his BMT so we still had to be cautious, even while in the states. Not to mention, Justin was still very, very weak. He could only walk a few steps without needing to sit down and rest. Remember how different trips are when it's just you versus when you have small children? You have to pack everything under the sun that they could possibly need everywhere you go. Well, planning a trip for Justin was the same except amplified. Forgetting something needed for a small child would result in discomfort or ending a day early. However, forgetting something for an ill kid could result in a trip to the emergency room or worse. We thought of everything when we packed for him: medications, tons of sunscreen, umbrellas to keep the sun off him, bandages, a wheelchair and everything in between. We were set to leave a few days after graduation and something happened to take the trip from good to amazing. Brady decided to come with us. It was a big gesture for him to forego his trip to Mexico with their friends and come to Florida with us. I knew Justin was his very best friend and it touched us all that Brady wanted to come.

"Justin and I became friends our sophomore year of high school. Since then he has been one of the best examples in my life and someone that I look up to the most. He has been through endless trials and countless hospital visits and yet he remains positive. Every time he has been pushed down he has gotten right back up and it is truly inspiring. It has been incredible to see him go through so much and to come out on top. He is one of the funniest guys I have ever met and I am convinced that he can quote any movie. He is my best friend, my go to man, and someone I strive to be like, but above all, he is my brother."— Brady

The trip was a long one and there were plenty of times that Justin felt awful. He was nauseated and fatigued most of the time but still smiling. It's amazing what we start to take as "normal" things. We just started to expect things that we grew accustomed to, like how sick he always felt. We did the Disney and the beach thing. Justin was in a wheelchair for all of Disney but he had his entire family there with him celebrating his life. He was overly hot a lot and we had to get inventive with ways to keep him cool. The beach was one of his favorite places to be. He was able to relax and had a sense of peace there. We had to keep him in the shade and be sure he was hydrated and cool enough but when all of those pieces came together, he felt content.

The month of May was a whirlwind. We were able to leave Houston and go home at the end of April and then Justin was hit with the state baseball tournament, graduating high school and a senior/family trip to Florida. When Justin was diagnosed we weren't sure if or when he would ever be able to do those things but there he was doing them. It was surreal almost.

CHAPTER 14

June 6th, picture it: It was MLB draft day and we were visiting family in North Carolina. I was upstairs at my parents' home in Charlotte, North Carolina giving my grandson a bath and Justin was downstairs watching TV. We were the only people home. My phone rang several times in a row but I couldn't get away from giving Tripp a bath so I just let it ring. As I was getting Tripp out of the tub and drying him off, I heard Justin scream so I grabbed Tripp and ran out to the balcony and yelled down to Justin to see if he was okay. He came into view with a combination of smiling and laughing and trying to catch his breath and said, "Guess who got drafted to the Rockies!" I breathed a sigh of relief that he was okay and then thought about the phone calls I'd received while I was bathing Tripp. I figured it must have been one of his good friends because he played ball with some guys who had amazing talent. I said, "Ohhhh who?!?" And with the biggest smile I'd ever seen he said, "ME!!!!!" Then it was me who couldn't catch *my* breath as I said, "No, no, no, no..." repeatedly. I started shaking and I whisked Tripp downstairs. I thought Justin was joking around. He was jumping up and down and laughing. His phone was beeping with text after text and ringing with phone calls and I just cried. As he stood there, he told me that a couple of his friends had called and told him. He showed me the pictures and showed me on the website what round he was drafted in. I'd spoken with a scout, Chris Forbes, for the Colorado Rockies a few days prior but I obviously had no idea what he was up to.

In an interview with the Denver Post, Forbes said, *"I gravitate toward people like Justin. Drafting him was a no-brainer for us. Baseball is a game about statistics and wins and losses, but this is bigger than that. This is an opportunity to lay a foundation for a kid. This is something he can hold onto forever. He can always say 'I was a 35th-rounder with the Rockies in 2012.' Baseball is a competitive business, but I will sleep well tonight knowing we drafted Justin."*

70

Since the beginning of this journey my faith in humanity had been restored ten times over. All we ever hear about is the pain, betrayal and hurt in any given situation so it was inspiring to see so much good.

As Justin's luck would seem to go, the good things came to an end as some things we didn't understand started to rear their head and we were on a plane back to Houston on June 11th. Justin was having a lot of diarrhea, nausea, abdominal pain and fatigue. We feared the worst as we flew back to the Houston hospital with the dread of gut GVHD (Graft Versus Host Disease). "GVHD is a condition that can develop after a bone marrow transplant. It happens when donor derived T-cells attack the recipient tissue."[8] We stayed in Houston for a week as Justin underwent a myriad of tests. He had his regular BMT appointment but also had a scope and stomach biopsy to try to figure out what was going on. We left North Carolina with Justin's grandfather in the hospital. He had an infection in his neck and had been in the hospital for a week. Though it was tough to leave right then, we also knew that we had to figure out what was going on with Justin. Life didn't stop. That just wasn't the case. Life continued on, people got sick, loved ones had other hurts and pain they were dealing with and every day we just did the best we could.

After a day of testing, Justin's counts all looked decent. His kidney levels were somewhat elevated but the doctors felt like that would straighten itself out with more fluid. His platelets dropped and they checked his chimerism to be sure he was 100% donor cells. If they were to detect any of Justin's own cells, it would mean that the transplant wasn't successful. As we waited for the results of the chimerism test, Justin prepared for his scope and biopsy the following day.

As I just mentioned, life didn't stop. Bad news didn't wait for a "good" time. While in Houston, we learned that Justin's great grandmother, the same wonderful woman we stayed with when Justin was released from the hospital weeks after his initial diagnosis, had been diagnosed with stage 4 colon cancer that had metastasized to her lungs and lymph nodes. On that very same day, Justin's great aunt was having brain surgery. Sometimes I just had to stop. I had to stop thinking and hearing. I had to stop talking and watching. I had to stop seeing and knowing. I just had to stop. I couldn't take everything in and process it anymore. I couldn't reach beyond the scope of whom and what was directly in front of me. It was too much. It was all too much and somehow my heart found a way to break in the midst of it already breaking.

After Justin's stomach procedures, the doctor said that they saw something in his upper stomach. They took several biopsies but we knew we would have to wait to hear the results. Even though I was worried, Justin came out of his sedation making jokes - always making jokes. It amazed me. The moments that I actually stopped to think about it left me stumped. The past year he had spent fighting for his life but he never really stopped smiling and laughing. Of course there were moments when he cried, when he was afraid or tired or in pain. But he just never stopped smiling. Ever. It was my job to care for him in every way possible: medically, emotionally, spiritually, etc. I tried to keep his spirits up but to be honest, that wasn't too hard most of the time. He always had that great attitude but enduring anything for too long can be taxing on anyone.

We flew back to New Mexico, where we were living at the time, and waited with bated breath for the test results. We waited and we waited. I called the hospital in Houston after a week had gone by but there were still no results. And on June 18th, I found myself getting on a plane for an entirely different reason. Not only was I getting on a plane but I was leaving Justin and that felt odd but it was for a wonderful cause. My oldest son, Jordan, was getting married. Life kept happening. While it was bad news for so long over and over, this was news I could handle. I was excited for Jordan and his soon-to-be wife. They had a son together so it just made sense. I didn't want to miss their wedding and I was appreciative that everything fell together in such a way that I was able to attend. Justin was up and down. He had his good days and his bad days and we were still on the, "Houston once a month for a checkup, Albuquerque twice a month to be sure everything was still moving in the right direction and Farmington once a month for labs" schedule but overall things seemed to be okay so I felt good about leaving for a few days.

CHAPTER 15

Initially we thought that we would be able to fly back to Houston from New Mexico for a period of time and then that would fizzle out and Justin would only have to be seen locally to monitor his labs. That was our intended direction. The cancer was in remission and Justin's new cells were growing. Albeit they were growing slowly but they were still growing nonetheless. Things were as "on track" as we would have imagined them to be. However, Justin's gut issues continued to be a problem and we realized fairly quickly that we were either going to have to move back to Houston for a period of time or continue flying back and forth. Both options were costly so I did some investigating. Living in Houston was hard not only because of cost but also because we didn't have any family or friends close by. The medical part was hard as it was but not having any support emotionally and mentally close by made everything that much more difficult. Never underestimate the power of personal connection. I believe it did more for Justin than any medication or treatment. My parents and older 2 children lived in Charlotte, North Carolina at the time so I looked into hospitals close to that area that were well known with good reputations. The two hospitals that I looked into were in the Durham/Chapel Hill area. Justin's BMT doctor in Houston recommended a doctor at a Durham hospital, Dr. Smith. We decided to set up an appointment and inspect the hospital and Dr. Smith. Justin was scheduled for a July 3rd appointment.

I remember pulling into the parking garage at the Durham hospital thinking about how "manageable" the hospital seemed. The Houston hospital was so vast. There were so many buildings and it was rightly a city in itself. The Durham hospital was different. It looked easier to navigate and less daunting. I will admit that I wondered if it would be as good as the Houston hospital because it was much smaller. Thank God Justin was still being seen in the children's hospital since he was diagnosed when he was sixteen. Everything was much brighter and more colorful. Dr. Smith had a great "rap sheet." He was well known for his work and highly recommended by his bone marrow transplant patients. He looked at all of Justin's medical records that I brought, accepted him as a patient if we were interested and then put him on a high dose of steroids because of his gut issues that everyone believed was GVHD. Our plan was to move to North Carolina by summer's end so Justin's care could be continued at the Durham hospital. Again, we naively believed that we could move out to North Carolina, live with my parents and get Justin care in Durham for a couple of months. Then when he was well enough and could move away, we could look at next steps. That was our plan.

What's that they say? Life is what happens when you're busy making other plans? We returned to New Mexico and within a couple of weeks of traveling to check out the hospital in Durham, Justin started peeing blood and was peeing frequently. His blood pressure started reading high as well. Rather than move in August, we decided to bump it up to July. It wasn't really a choice. We had to leave immediately. We arrived in Charlotte late in the evening and Justin had an appointment the following day. The airplane ride was extremely difficult as Justin had to pee every 20 minutes and it was red with blood and painful every time. The Durham hospital was a 2 hour drive from Charlotte so we stocked up on pee funnels before we left. We started out toward Durham the following morning and Justin immediately made use of his first pee funnel. He was in the front seat so he would get on his knees and turn around in the seat to pee in the funnel. He had a great deal of discomfort that would alleviate somewhat once he peed. That was the routine for the following 2 hours. Arriving at the hospital in Durham, we made our way to the children's bone marrow transplant floor. Justin was taken back to the day hospital where they ran blood and urine tests on him. After seeing the degree of his pain as well as the blood in his urine, they admitted him. We moved over to the 5th floor, the Bone Marrow Transplant inpatient floor, of the main hospital. The doctors still weren't sure what was going on with him but they knew they had to admit him while they ran tests to try to figure it out. Little did we know that it would become one of Justin's longest hospital stays.

CHAPTER 16

The following day Justin was still peeing blood and in a lot of pain. He had blood clots in his bladder and his blood pressure continued to be high. He was still peeing every 20 minutes indicating that his bladder was spasming, making him feel like he needed to pee but he would only expel a little bit each time. The doctors thought that he had a virus in his bladder that was causing it to bleed; in turn, it was causing all of his platelets to go to the site to try to clot the blood and left him needing more platelets. He started receiving 2 platelet transfusions a day. They thought he got the virus because he was started on steroids, which further suppressed his already compromised immune system. In addition, he had another issue: his kidneys weren't functioning well so they ordered a biopsy of his kidneys and GI tract. The following couple days showed that Justin did have BK Virus in his bladder. The doctors explained that his kidneys were only operating at 25% - if that. He was holding onto waste and his creatinine was 2.1, double what it should have been. It seemed that all of his cells were getting eaten up and destroyed. A nephrologist (kidney doctor), Dr. Reynolds, was called in to help with Justin's case. Dr. Reynolds thought that Justin had Atypical HUS, an extremely rare, life-threatening, progressive disease. "Atypical Hemolytic-Uremic Syndrome is a syndrome characterized by three major problems areas: 1) progressive renal failure 2) problems associated with red blood cell and platelet counts and 3) problems that occur in the vascular system."[9] We were terrified that this might be the case. I begged everyone I knew to pray it wasn't. Justin had been through so much. We didn't want to add complete kidney failure to that list. I couldn't even imagine it. One night, in the first week in the hospital, he needed both blood and platelets and his body actually became overloaded with fluid. Because they overloaded his system so badly, they changed his parameters for receiving blood and platelets. They changed his platelet parameter to

30k so if he were to fall below 30k, he would get a transfusion. That morning his platelets were at 31k but he was having bad nosebleeds so they went ahead and transfused. By the next morning he was coughing badly and needed oxygen, and as the day progressed his cough became worse and he became extremely lethargic. An X-ray showed that he had fluid in his right lung - possible pneumonia. It was literally one thing right after another. I actually take that back, sometimes it wasn't even right after another. Often things got piled on simultaneously. He just couldn't catch a break. We were waiting on several tests (his FISH test and kidney biopsy) to come back to try to get a better picture of what was going on inside Justin's body. That day someone asked Justin, "Do you believe that God can heal you?" Justin's response: "I believe He already has."

Do you ever just stare at someone and wonder how they acquired such faith, perseverance and will? That wasn't the first time I looked at Justin that way. It touched me deeply to hear him talk with such faith. It made me ashamed sometimes that I questioned so much. I was quickly realizing that maybe Justin was teaching me more in his short life than I had ever taught him.

At the hospital, along the counter at the nurses' station, there are file holders that are numbered and correspond to the patient's room. I picked up the print out of Justin's labs every morning. It almost seemed like buying a lottery ticket. I never knew if we would win and get good news, or at least not bad news, or if I would cringe going over his lab results. I became decently proficient at reading and understanding his labs. Of course, I asked a million questions along the way to get to that point. And honestly, we got more bad news than good most of the time. Every time I went to grab the print out, I worried. His labs from the next morning terrified me. His creatinine had gone up to 2.6. We didn't have any official test results though so I tried to remain calm until we heard something. But truth be told, I was a mess. I thought we were past the serious part of the whole process, but we were realizing that the complications that can potentially come from a BMT can be more serious and life threatening than the cancer itself. It was hard to remember ever feeling so scared. When Justin started feeling so much better, the devastation I'd felt when he was so sick was soon covered by gratitude. With all the new developments and life threatening issues that arose once again, I was finding it hard to remember how to breathe. I had no control over my body. I would cry and not be able to stop. I always tried to go into the bathroom or out into the hospital's family room when I felt it coming. It came like a wave, slowly at first and then crushing. The thoughts behind the tears, the fear that lay at the corners of my mind brought me to my knees. Again, I would use my shower time as a release. It was the best place to let go. I could cry and let the water wash my tears down the drain. And with each gasp for breath, I prayed. I begged and I pleaded with God.

I felt like God couldn't have possibly brought Justin to this point without a plan for him. I didn't understand it, any of it, but I had hope and hope is an amazing thing.

There's something to be said about losing yourself and in doing so discovering who you really are. Or maybe it's just discovering another layer, another version of you. Perhaps it was there all along but you never had a need for it until tragedy struck. It's in those grim times, those gut-wrenching, soul crushing times that you find out what you're really made of. I also found the true meaning of the word, "faith." There's a quote somewhere that says, "Faith isn't faith until it's all you're holding onto." I don't know that I've ever found anything to be more true. When everything is stripped away and all odds point to the worst outcome, all you have is faith. You cling to that tighter than you've ever held onto anything in your life. You clutch it with bloody hands and a tired heart and you just don't let go.

I lost time in a sense while Justin was in the hospital. The days bled into each other. Sleep was something that became a luxury. We were in a hospital room all day, every day but we kept busy with his care and the many tests they ran on him. He was still getting platelet transfusions every day and sometimes blood transfusions. Justin felt too crappy to watch TV and once in a while I would turn the TV on and realize how long it had been since I watched anything. I had no idea what TV shows were airing and the ones I knew about I wasn't following. Justin was in a great deal of pain a lot of the time because of the BK Virus. He had to push through one blood clot after another when he peed. Sometimes I would walk in the bathroom and it looked like someone had been violently attacked as there was blood everywhere. When your body feels like it's crashing, like it's just decided it has had enough, it doesn't take long for your mind to get on board with that. I talked to Justin about his good memories in hopes of overriding the painful ones that were quickly adding up. We talked about the good times amidst the bad. I wanted him to remember that even though he felt it was all pain and bad feedback, we had some great times in all of those moments in between.

CHAPTER 17

I never really left Justin. Sure I would go take a shower or walk down the hall for ice; I would even go downstairs to pick up food that my dear friend, Paige, would drop off. So many people told me that I needed to go and rest, as least for one solid night but I couldn't leave him. I'm sure they were right. I'm sure it would have done my system good to rest but I would have been too worried about him. I watched him sleep and I would touch him often so he knew he wasn't alone. It became routine for me to check for a fever when I walked by him as he rested. I never had to stare death in the face before all of this - not with myself or anyone else. I found myself soaking in every part of him. Etching his face, his hands, his laugh into my memory.

Days came and went with no real change. Doctors did every test under the sun, including ordering a lung biopsy and a bronchoscopy, trying to figure out what was going on in his lungs. They cancelled the lung biopsy as his blood and platelets were just too low and they worried about him bleeding during the procedure. Testing showed that pneumonia was occupying Justin's entire right lung and he was put on two more antibiotics, in addition to the one he was already on, making a total of three. The doctor also saw that his lung was bloody because his platelets were so low and when he coughed, it caused the capillaries to burst and bleed. They were *also* worried about a fungal infection so they put him on an anti-fungal medication that wasn't hard on his kidneys. Justin's FISH test came back showing that he was still 100% donor cells, which was the only good news amidst so much bad. The BK Virus in Justin's bladder started to get better and then got very bad again and stayed that way. He continued to pee large amounts of blood and had very hefty clots that he had to pass, which continued to be incredibly painful for him. All signs were pointing to the fact that Justin *did* have Atypical HUS, which continued to damage his kidneys. It was destroying his platelets and red blood cells faster than his body could produce them so Justin was getting transfusions twice a day. After the doctors at the Durham hospital conferred with the doctors in Houston, they decided to start him on a process called plasmapheresis which is essentially taking out all of his plasma and replacing it with new, healthy plasma. "Your blood comes out through one of the tubes and goes into a machine that separates your plasma from your blood cells. Then your blood cells get mixed with fresh plasma, and the new blood mixture goes back into your body through the other tube."[10] Once they started, we hoped to see an increase in kidney function and that it was just a matter of time until we could get things back on track on for him.

I stood back sometimes and tried to take it all in. I tried to wrap my mind around everything and tried to make sense out of any of it. I couldn't. I learned that all I could do was try to handle the moment that was right in front of me. The trick was to tackle that current moment while making sure I knew where Justin was headed.

On a lighter note, on one of those long nights, Justin got me laughing again. He was sleeping but with all of the meds he was on, his sleep was rough and his dream state often continued after he appeared to be awake. He started to move around and was talking in his sleep as his covers slipped off of him. I went over to cover him back up and I bent down to ask him if he was okay to which he replied: "Mom, I don't have my Valentine's list"...and then he promptly asked for a popsicle. Oh how I laughed and then cried with thankfulness that I get to be his momma.

Justin's days fluctuated. One day he seemed to be doing much better and the next, he was worse. It was the whole "one step forward, two steps back" thing. Now that we were at the hospital in Durham, it was easier to have family and friends visit. My parents made a trip to see us. They brought Justin video games which made him happy for a time. It was always good to see familiar faces and they did lift our spirits. There was always that point though, when they had to go home and Justin and I were still there. Justin still felt terrible and there was no end in sight. It was frustrating and it started to wear on Justin mentally. He was 3 ½ weeks into his current hospital stay and was slipping into depression. I went out in the hall and found a nurse to ask the inpatient doctor to come talk to me. He did and I expressed my worry over Justin's mental well-being. The doctor looked at his records again, went over his labs and then said that I could take him out of the hospital on a 4 hour pass. That was such a big deal and I knew that stepping outside those hospital walls would do Justin so much good. Of course, he would have to take his urine drainage bag as he had a catheter but it was worth figuring out. I knew that Justin couldn't do anything taxing as he was so weak and still felt bad so I thought that a movie sounded perfect. That was our first outing, a trip to the movie theater to see *Batman*. He was that good kind of tired afterwards and had the best sleep he'd had since before he was admitted. His BK Virus was still a problem but his spirits were definitely better.

After days and days of needing blood and platelet transfusions twice a day and Justin's creatinine level going back up, the doctors decided to start plasmapheresis. Justin was worried that it wouldn't work and we were quickly running out of options. Plasmapheresis was a long process. Justin's blood pressure went up even more and his calcium decreased so they had to give him more calcium during the process. They decided that he would have plasmapheresis every day for a while until they could determine if it was helping. In addition, they did a GFR (Glomerular Filtration Rate) study on him to determine exactly how his kidneys were functioning. "Glomerular filtration rate (GFR) is a test used to check how well the kidneys are working. Specifically, it estimates how much blood passes through the glomeruli each minute. Glomeruli are the tiny filters in the kidneys that filter waste from the blood."[11] They did this because they wanted to start a medicine (Cidofovir) that would help his bladder with the BK virus (that wasn't improving at all) but that same medicine is very hard on the kidneys. After completing the GFR study, they decided against giving him Cidofovir because his kidneys wouldn't be able to handle it. The next day he had an ultrasound on his bladder before his next round of plasmapheresis. If and when his kidneys started to improve, they could start the Cidofovir.

Days 2 and 3 of plasmapheresis were tough. They popped one of his veins and then it took them two more tries to get the needle in. It's a very large needle so it was painful for Justin. His calcium decreased again, making his hand cramp and face tingle. They had to supplement his calcium, giving him more as they did the pheresis. His sugar climbed to 345 and he started shaking a lot. His blood pressure continued to be high. He had to have blood and platelet transfusions that night. His creatinine went up instead of down like we had hoped. A plus, though, was that his lungs cleared up almost entirely. We took any victory we could get and that was actually a big one.

As his days continued to tick by, Justin was destroying his blood and platelets at an alarming rate and couldn't seem to stay caught up making them. It seemed like it was actually getting worse. He would have another day of plasmapheresis and then get a couple of days off to get IVIG (Intravenous Immunoglobulin). IVIG is given to people with weakened immune systems to fight off infections. We were hoping it would aide in fighting off his infections so we could get Justin well.

CHAPTER 18

Justin spent his 18th birthday in the hospital. Family services went out of their way to throw him a birthday party with Bull from the Durham Bulls baseball team. Justin was wheeled in a wheelchair, gowned and masked up, into the family room decorated with balloons made from doctors' gloves and a cake. Friends he made on the BMT floor surrounded the table, including his best pal, Brian, a 5 year old who was in the room beside his. It wasn't what I pictured. It wasn't what I imagined for his 18th birthday. It was sterile but still warm somehow. There was far too much sickness and pain in that one room on the 5th floor of a hospital tucked into the lush countryside of Durham, North Carolina, but there was so much love there too - love of family, new friends, nurses and doctors who took Justin into their hearts and hands. It wasn't what we imagined but it was another birthday and for that we were grateful.

The day after his birthday, the doctors put a double lumen Vas-Cath in his chest. They placed it because of all of the IV medications Justin was taking. It was easier to get him what he needed with more entry points. In addition, he had a three-way Foley catheter placed, which is for irrigation and drainage of his bladder. His BK Virus was so bad and he was losing so much blood that they felt like they needed to hurry and get a handle on things. There was a catheter that went up his penis and into his bladder that was used to irrigate and drain the bladder. There was an opening in the catheter tube on the outside of his body that the nurses could use to push fluid into his bladder and then pull it back out if blood clots got stuck. I was on the BMT floor waiting for Justin to come back from the catheter placement surgery. I had confetti in hand getting ready to throw it up in the air as a child was being discharged from the hospital, to wish her farewell. Right before we were to release the confetti, I saw Justin in the sanitation room getting ready to come through the second set of doors back onto the unit and he looked to be in a tremendous amount of pain. Naturally, I handed my confetti off to a social worker standing beside me and made my way to Justin. I can honestly say that I'd never seen him in such intense, acute pain. I was under the assumption that the catheter would alleviate most of his pain from passing those blood clots but the pain he was in after having the catheter inserted far surpassed anything I'd ever seen with him. They got him into the room and gave him more pain meds as they could see he absolutely needed them. They knew that a clot he was unable to pass was the cause for the pain so they immediately tried to irrigate him. A wonderful nurse worked over him feverishly pushing fluid in and pulling back. While she could push the fluid in, she couldn't pull any back out. You can imagine how that would only add to and intensify his pain. With one hand he was gripping the side rail of the bed - the other hand firmly clasped the button that released his pain meds. He had tears streaming down his face as he begged me to help him. That feeling of helplessness was all encompassing. There was absolutely nothing I could do. I asked the nurses and doctors to give him more pain meds. I held his hand. I stroked his head but ultimately I was absolutely helpless. At one point, I even asked the doctor to put him out, completely under because I didn't know how much longer he could handle that kind of pain. The nurse continued to work hard to rid him of his agony and then all of a sudden, after endless minutes of uninterrupted pain, it stopped and his entire body relaxed. He let go of everything. He went limp as his eyes rolled up and closed and he fell asleep. The nurse finally had success. She had sucked the culprit clot out and in doing so alleviated Justin's suffering. There was a time when I couldn't imagine anything being worse than him having cancer and the treatment that accompanied that but now this seemed to trump anything I'd seen him go through. Or maybe it just felt like that.

Over the next week, Justin held his ground. All in all, he was about the same. They did an ultrasound on his bladder and the clot in his bladder had decreased significantly but was still rather large. They felt confident that irrigating his bladder with the Foley catheter was helping. His kidneys were the same as they had been. Plasmapheresis was being done three times a week. He was still getting platelets twice a day but only needed blood once a day so that was an improvement. And then a couple of days later, things took a turn for the worse again. Justin's creatinine level jumped up to 3.0, dangerously high. The doctors decided to go back to plasmapheresis every day. They were baffled as to what was going on with his kidneys. Of the 17+ pounds of fluid weight Justin had put on in 5 days, he shed about 5 of those pounds in one day, thanks to Lasix (used to reduce extra fluid in the body). However, Lasix also hurts the kidneys. Everything was a balancing act. We learned that early on when he was getting chemo. Treatments, medications and procedures that can help one thing tend to hurt something else. Again, it was risk versus risk, a familiar concept.

That dance continued over the following week. One day things looked better and we thought Justin was on his way to recovery and then we would hit a snag and be sent backwards. An ultrasound showed that his kidneys were still large and hadn't shrunk, which was a positive sign that they would be able to recover at some point so that was definitely good news. The nurses continued to irrigate Justin regularly. For most of the nurses it was their first time doing something like that. They usually caught on quickly and were able to alleviate Justin's pain of the wedged blood clots. I remember one night Justin's nurse didn't have any experience with irrigation and just kind of threw caution to the wind. He tried and tried but couldn't get the clot to move and the harder he tried, the more Justin hurt. Finally, I whipped open the door and saw one of his regular nurses standing in the hall. I felt bad for asking because I knew she was busy with her other patients but I didn't know what to do as Justin was in a great deal of pain. I asked her if she would come help and she immediately came over, gowned up and took over. I saw her eyes when she walked in the room. There was blood everywhere, along with syringes and paper towels. Within just a few minutes, she rescued Justin from his pain and he was able to rest again. Justin was able to get rid of a lot of the fluid he was retaining over the next few days so we felt like maybe his kidneys were healing. The doctors also took the catheter out that he'd had in for weeks and Justin was incredibly happy about that. We thought that things were looking up and like we were definitely headed in the right direction.

Of course, some warped version of the hokey pokey ensued and it was another 3 steps back for Justin. He started running a fever. The doctors started him on antibiotics and ran a myriad of cultures. In addition, we got the results back from the BK Virus test they sent off for detection of BK in the bladder and in the blood stream. The virus was still over 5 billion strong in the bladder and had jumped to over 6,000 in the blood stream. By that time it had been 6 weeks that Justin was fighting that damned BK Virus. Because of Justin's kidney issues, the doctors couldn't treat it like they normally would so everything was worse and it was taking much longer to heal. We started to wonder if it ever would. On top of all of that, the catheter that was pulled out had to essentially be put back in. They did an ultrasound and found the clot to be as big as it always had been. They didn't know if it just never decreased, which would be hard to believe with as much manual irrigating as those wonderful nurses had been doing, or if it just got that much worse in the past two days. Justin was in pain before they put the catheter back in because he had a clot and couldn't pee so at least he was able to get some relief with the catheter back in. He ran a high fever all night and was miserable. He was shaking and nauseated and couldn't relax so they gave him Ativan, which helped him rest for a while. In addition, the nephrologist came by concerned that the plasmapheresis wasn't working. It was punch after punch. You know how boxers train on that little punching bag that hangs down? It's kind of tricky, at least it looks that way, because they have to time it just right and roll their punches. Well we felt like Justin was that small hanging punching bag and it was literally a roll of punches, one right after another. I didn't know how, when or if the punches would stop coming and if they did, I didn't know if Justin would still be standing.

When they put a catheter in again, they put in a different kind of catheter because it was supposed to work better than the previous one, even though that one worked fine. They then pulled that catheter out because a clot was stuck and couldn't be passed and once again Justin came off the bed in pain. They then put the same type catheter he had previously *back* in, which would make catheter #3. No rest for the weary. Justin and I were up all night the next night. He ended up having both of the catheters that were inserted, removed. Neither worked. They got clogged with clots and nothing could be extracted. We finally tried to sleep around 5:30 AM but that didn't last. Justin's bladder had been spasming badly so they put him on Valium to help. The urologist was supposed to come by that evening to discuss taking him to the operating room and evacuating his bladder. In addition, they were discussing injecting Cidofovir directly into his bladder to try to help with the BK Virus while bypassing the kidneys. They did some research to see if anyone had ever tried putting it directly into the bladder. They had a protocol for that and it sounded as though it was something they would try but we weren't sure yet. His creatinine had climbed once again to 3.1. Plasmapheresis was cancelled again because of his fever. His cultures showed a gram positive bacterium in his blood but they weren't sure exactly what it was. Justin was absolutely exhausted. They finally made the decision to give him the first dose of Cidofovir. The nurse inserted the medication directly into his bladder through his catheter and then clamped the catheter for an hour to contain the treatment. After that hour they removed the catheter.

That night, Justin was in inconsolable, excruciating pain all night long and well into the next morning. He finally got relief, after endless hours, when they inserted catheter #4 and irrigated. Seeing him hurt like that and watching him take one hit after another finally took its toll and it broke me. I don't like for Justin to see me cry so I stepped into the bathroom but what took place when I heard that door click into place, knowing it was secure and closed, was scary. I hardly got the door closed in time before a plea escaped my lips as tears exploded from my eyes. I felt the fear and the pain and the anger in my gut. It started in my stomach and leached out until it twisted every organ and pricked every single nerve. It took me to my knees and I cried so hard I was gasping for breath. And then I prayed. No, I don't know if I would call what I was doing "praying." I begged God, I pleaded with Him bartering my soul to help Justin. I beseeched Him to alleviate his pain and to help him heal. I asked Him to tell me what to do, assuring Him that I would do anything. And then I was instantly calmed. I felt a peace come over me as I kept hearing the same words over and over again in my head, "Trust Me." Just two words. Only two. But those two words jerked me out of the panic I so quickly flew into. Those two words enveloped my mind and wrapped around my body to quiet the screams and stop the shaking. God wanted me to trust in Him, to trust in His plan. I lifted my head, eyes swollen above a tear sodden face and I just breathed. As I stood up, I knew what I had to do.

I wrapped my hand around the door handle, flung the door open and told Justin, "Today is the day we start turning things around so get ready. You are getting up out of the bed and we are going on a walk." He just looked at me and started to argue. All he wanted to do was stay in bed as his current condition was starting to wear on his mind and heart. I told him that he could decide when but it needed to be in the next couple of hours. And he did so - begrudgingly. Justin had been in the hospital by that time for over 6 weeks but from that moment on there was no more waiting around for something to happen. We were going to make things happen. We were going to walk and exercise and eat right and pray and have the mindset of being well and healthy.

CHAPTER 19

Day 2 of the official "turnaround" started off a bit bleak. Justin started the day with plasmapheresis. He didn't sleep well the night before so I was happy to see him sleep through plasmapheresis. His creatinine, while still high, did come down a little bit. He also had a chest X-ray that morning that showed that the pneumonia had gotten worse in his right lung. More meds were started and they ordered a CT scan. He was in a great deal of pain from the spasms he had the other night and he was scheduled to get his second dose of Cidofovir directly into his bladder. Things didn't look better per se but I guess the difference was *hope*. The day before I was at my breaking point and had misplaced my hope but I had since gotten it back. Hope makes more of a difference than I had realized.

By the third day we started to see some changes. After 2 doses of Cidofovir, Justin's bladder seemed to be on the mend. I couldn't believe it. His creatinine dropped significantly. We had tried everything before and I was thankful to his brilliant medical team and God's guidance that they tried the Cidofovir in his bladder. On another note, we did have a slight bump - a slight delay. Justin's pneumonia had gotten worse. It was now in both lungs and the Infectious Disease doctors were called in.

Justin's bladder continued to show signs of improvement so they pulled his catheter the following day. He was able to be disconnected from his IV pole so we went on a walk around the floor. He needed to be up and moving around with his pneumonia getting worse. Not to mention, staying in bed all day is a direct road to depression. That's why we were thankful for his day passes. He developed a crack in his PICC line so they pulled that as well. Normally they would replace it but they didn't think he needed it anymore. Justin continued that dance over the next couple of days. One thing would look better and something else would be worse. He got blood and platelet transfusions regularly still. His bladder and pneumonia finally improved simultaneously and aside from the 20 pounds of fluid that Justin was retaining and severe nausea, things looked to be on the right track.

I used to want to travel abroad and live among, to learn about, other cultures. I never imagined that I would have that opportunity to do just that there on the BMT floor of the Durham hospital. There were families there from India and Qatar and the one thing I learned was that love really is the universal language. Smiles and kindness transcend any cultural boundaries and are appreciated in any language. I spoke to both of those families and both were kind and genuine. Sharaa, from Qatar, wouldn't let me pass by without giving me whatever she had. If she was eating, she would take some off her own plate to give to me. She spoke little to no English and I certainly didn't speak Arabic, although I do know how to say a few words now, but we were able to communicate somehow. It's amazing how crisis can bring people together. Crisis brings about clarity and shows us what is important. It strips away everything and leaves you raw and your vision untainted. We were there at the Durham hospital for a common purpose, to help our children get well. In doing so, we all learned valuable lessons that extended far beyond the walls of a hospital.

It seemed like the more I started speaking positively about Justin's progress, the better he did. He still did that 2 steps forward, 1 step back dance but he was slowly moving forward still. The installments of Cidofivir in his bladder were helping greatly. The two things that were the hardest to get under control at that point were his pneumonia and his severe nausea. Because his nausea was terrible, it was hard for him to get the nourishment he needed to help in getting well. It was very difficult for him to stay hydrated as well which made us worry more about his bladder and keeping it flushed. They put him back on Budesonide which seemed to help with his nausea. In addition, they continued with his plasmapheresis as well as X-rays to watch the progress of the pneumonia. Another week went by and we were approaching the end of September. Justin had been in the hospital for over 2 months that go-round. We wondered if the leaves were changing in the mountains or if there was a chill in the air that pricked at your skin when you walked outside. Justin's day passes were hit and miss depending how well he was doing on a given day. Not too long before, there was a day when his sister came to visit and we went out on a day pass and it got scary quickly. Justin was on a lot of pain medication because of that blood clot in his bladder. On one particular day when we went on pass he started to get terrible withdrawals. He was shaking like crazy and throwing up. After that day, we rarely left the hospital. As fall started to roll in just beyond our window pane, we imagined what the air would feel like on our skin. We wondered if we would need a jacket yet as we watched the trees pitch slowly in the chilled breeze.

Ever since that day I spent on bended knee in the bathroom, I tried to remain positive amidst all the negativity. The reality was that Justin's body just couldn't get moving in a positive direction. There was always something holding it back. Lately it was his lungs. There were several days we thought they would release us but X-rays would show fluid in or around his lungs and so we stayed. And we waited. Every day I was reminded of the life that was quite literally passing us by. We watched it do so from his hospital room. We watched his friends in college playing baseball. We watched as they went on dates and took vacations. We watched as his nephew grew. We watched as his brother and his wife made their life, working hard and raising their son. We watched as the nurses came in with stories of their families and we watched as some nurses came and went. We watched the season change and we waited for Justin's turn to rejoin and become an active participant in his life.

And then I wondered if we could just try it. What if they discharged Justin and we stayed close? What if we gave his mind and body the gift of life outside the hospital? I watched how having his friends around making him happy directly impacted his health. Maybe being able to get out of that hospital and sit on a real couch, eat at a kitchen table and not be connected to tubes tethered to a pole would make a difference. I bargained with the doctors. I begged them to just try it, promising to stay at the Ronald McDonald House right by the hospital for a while. And they agreed.

CHAPTER 20

After being hospitalized for 2+ months, Justin was released and we made our way to the Ronald McDonald House. As we walked outside, the sunlight almost felt strange - strange but glorious. We just stood there, Justin's arm was draped over my shoulders for support and we raised our faces to the sky. He was very happy to be out of the hospital but exhausted so we went inside to rest. The Ronald McDonald House was one bedroom with 2 full beds, a kitchen, living room and a washer and dryer. We felt like kings. Everything is relative. Our lives had changed so much in just over a year. We went from a normal life living at home to a life of hospitals, RMH, apartments and hotels. We learned early on how to appreciate the simple things, from chairs to couches to beds.

Justin went back to the hospital the following 2 days for labs, a chest X-ray and plasmapheresis. He had been getting platelet transfusions daily, and sometimes twice a day, for almost 2 months, in addition to red blood cells. His need for red blood cells decreased a couple of weeks before he was released and he was only being transfused weekly. When we went in the day after he was discharged and saw his labs, we were shocked to see that although his platelets were dropping, he didn't need a transfusion. Heading to the hospital the next day, I told Justin that his appointment would probably be even longer because plasmapheresis would take a few hours and then he would more than likely need a platelet transfusion. To my surprise and utter joy, not only did Justin not need a transfusion but his platelets were actually going up! That hadn't been the case since early July. His urine was still clear and the X-ray showed that his lungs looked better!!! We decided to head home to Charlotte that day right after plasmapheresis knowing that Justin would have to be back on Friday.

That following week, we went back to Durham for labs and plasmapheresis. We also got Justin established at an oncology clinic in

Charlotte so he would have care close by. We still made frequent trips to Durham and Justin's labs continued to be of concern to his doctors and myself. The doctors started to feel as though plasmapheresis wasn't working after all. Justin's creatinine and LDH (lactate dehydrogenase which is used to check for tissue damage) were both climbing again. A normal LDH is around 105-250. "LDH is often used to check for tissue breakdown since it is abundant in red blood cells and can be a marker for hemolysis (the rupturing of red blood cells and release of their contents into surrounding fluid)."[12] They discussed beginning an experimental drug on him the following week, Solaris. Solaris is exceedingly expensive, $40,000 per dose, so they were waiting to see what they could do with insurance. It also increases susceptibility to life-threatening and fatal meningococcal infections so they were going to give Justin a vaccine to protect him.

The couple times a week to Durham quickly became a daily trip we made. Justin and I talked about everything under the sun in between moments of him dozing off to sleep. I was always taken back by how strong and mature he was. He was the perfect mixture of his father and me in his looks but he had a heart and mind that made me think of an old, wise soul. He was stronger than I could ever dream of being and often it was him comforting me during the trying times. His faith and his hope were awe-inspiring. I remember a conversation we had around that time. We were just talking freely and I said, "There is just so much going on right now. God thinks we can handle it but I just don't know," to which Justin quickly replied, "I think we can, mom." And *that* was the difference. His attitude of triumph and his perseverance in the midst of continuous strife was what set him apart. I was thankful for those moments. A very special friend and a former principal used to send us inspirational quotes in her weekly messages. In one she simply said, "Be present." I have since thought about those two words in depth and the significance they have had in my life. Be present. BE in the moments you are in. Experience them. Live inside them and absorb every particle of existence. Those moments, when you add them together, are your life. Be present for your life. Be thankful and enjoy the pieces that make up the puzzle. Those drives to Durham weren't how I would have chosen to spend time with my son but I learned that they were the most precious moments I could have asked for. We bonded in ways we wouldn't have if things were any different. Despite the situation, I grew to love those drives.

We tried to do a lot of living in those moments between hospital visits. Of course that would all depend on how Justin was feeling and he was often nauseated and always fatigued. We had a wheelchair we took everywhere because even walking wore him out. On one particular day we got to go to and participate in the Be The Match 5K run. We were thankful that we were able to come together for such a great cause and event. That was Jenna and my first 5K, I didn't run it – pushing Justin in a wheelchair uphill is tough in and of itself. Justin was worn out and had some swelling so he spent the rest of the day lying down, trying to rest. He was scheduled to go back to Durham the next day and, from my understanding, was going to begin that new medication, Solaris. We were praying it would set things straight for Justin's kidneys and that his body would stop destroying his cells. The beginning weeks of October brought more doctors' appointments as well as Justin's new medication. When we went to the hospital in Durham for a Solaris infusion, he always had to stay at least an hour so they could monitor him. In addition, he almost always had to get a platelet and/or blood transfusion. His creatinine was up to 3.5 and his LDH was over 1000. The test only measures to 1000 so we had some figuring out to do. The doctor decided that he would have to go see a nephrologist to formulate a plan. My heart ached. I was worried he would have to have dialysis. I fought and prayed with everything I had that this wasn't the case but it was looking like more and more of a possibility. I was determined and I was exercising the heck out of my faith. I adopted the idea that if I just believed enough, he would improve. If I just stuck by my guns and didn't falter, then God would see how vigilant I was and Justin would make a turn for the better. How do I show faith? It's one thing to say you have faith when everything is going okay for the most part, but what about when everything falls completely apart? Sometimes I wondered if I was being tested. I just believed that Justin would pull out of that lull. I believed that his kidneys would heal and he wouldn't need to be put on dialysis. And I rode that belief almost into the ground.

Justin reminded me quite frequently that despite how sick he felt most of the time, that kid with that brilliant sense of humor was still in there. I remember once when we got home from the hospital my parents were watching The Walking Dead marathon. We caught a snippet of one of the episodes where a guy was asking to stay on the farm and disclosed that his wife was pregnant. Justin then said: "Why are they having sex when there are zombies running around?!" He made jokes and laughed often regardless of the battle his body was fighting. And I admired him in every single way at any given moment - the way he bore the pain with grace, the way he joked with the doctors and nurses seconds after they gave him bad news, the way he cried when he was spent, but mostly I admired the way he fought. He fought for his life with more integrity and poise than most of us could muster on a normal day. He even woke up from sleep gracefully. On another early morning when we were heading to Durham, Justin surprised me again. He often nodded off to sleep because he was always so tired. I started stressing over traffic at one point when he was sleeping and he reached over and put his hand on my arm. He simply reached out and calmed my heart. He didn't say a word; he just touched me and left his hand on my arm for a while.

CHAPTER 21

And so the arduous road continued. Justin had many appointments at the hospital in Durham but on one visit about 10 days later we received some important information. Justin's platelets were at 18k on that visit so he received a transfusion. His red blood was okay at 10k (they were transfusing anything under 8k) but was continuing to drop. His LDH and creatinine were still as high as ever so the doctors had to decide if he should continue on the Solaris. He had his 4th dose the day before, making a month that he'd been on that medication. It didn't appear to be working but the doctors wanted a week to decide what they should do. Justin was an enigma, a puzzle, and they were trying to find that missing piece that would make everything make sense and set everything right. His cellularity was also of great concern. He was only about 20% cellular, where he should have been 80%. The cellularity of the bone marrow tells how much of the space inside the bone is filled with healthy, productive cells. Justin was making too few cells. They were going to recheck his cellularity a month later and if it didn't improve, they would very likely go back to the donor for more cells.

Time marched on and by the last week in October, I started running to help with all of the stress and anxiety I was feeling. It was also a time that I just cried. All in all, it was a good release. I finished my run one morning and sat down on the steps to the house. I had my iPod on and I just sat there as I continued to cry. I stared across the street and focused in on this particular tree. Many of its leaves had fallen but quite a few still remained. There was this one leaf near the bottom that was twirling around and dancing in the light breeze. I watched it for a while and then noticed that I couldn't see what was connecting it to the tree. To me, it appeared as though it was there all on its own, almost making fun of the breeze trying to pull it away from the tree. I knew though that wasn't true and that just because I couldn't see what was holding it there, didn't mean it wasn't there. I thought of Justin and how I knew that God was holding him even if sometimes I couldn't see him doing so. I thought of how Justin was fighting on and making fun of this cancer and all of its complications that were trying to pull him down. I knew that God was holding him in place and that although he was down, he had not fallen.

Justin's visit to the hospital in Durham that following week was a long one. I guess that's why I appreciated those moments of reprieve. They were welcomed and helped me refocus and get centered again. We were at the hospital all day. His platelets had bottomed out again so he got a transfusion. His creatinine and LDH levels were the same - high. He had his 5th infusion of Solaris and we were thinking that would be his last one as it didn't seem to be helping him. His eyes were affected by an infection or something but we wouldn't know what until some tests and studies came back. The doctor wanted to wait to begin medication to treat his eye issue until they knew what it was as any medication they gave him would affect him negatively. One medicine would hurt his kidneys while another would wipe out his immune system so we had to wait and see what the tests showed. On top of all of that, his vision was poor. He even fell that day before we left for his doctor appointment as he couldn't see very well and then didn't have the strength in his lower body to catch himself. Another test showed that his IGG (immunoglobulins) level was way low. We were going to have to drive back to Durham the following day so he could get IVIG to help fight off infections.

By then I'd learned a few things: take a shower when you can, eat and sleep when able and talk and love as much as possible. You just never know when you will lose the opportunity to do things or when those opportunities, which often turned into luxuries, would be put off for God knows how long. November 6th was a long day at the hospital; tests and infusions kept getting piled on and we got lost in the push and pull. We were all over the hospital and didn't know if we were coming or going. Justin had to get platelets, again. He was back to getting them every other day. He then went to see the eye doctor who thought that Justin's eye issues were tied to the Atypical HUS. He said that Justin was the only person in the world, as a BMT patient, who had this. He wasn't sure what would help or what would work for Justin's eyes because he'd never dealt with it before in that capacity. He went on to say that Justin's vision may be in jeopardy. A week before, Justin got a steroid shot in his eye to try to help with the swelling and with the blockages in the vessels in his eye and it *had* helped. After that visit with the eye doctor, we went back to the Day Hospital and Justin received an IVIG infusion. His blood pressure was tremendously high the day before as well so we had to wait for that to come down before we could leave. It was so late that we just grabbed a room at a hotel and went home the following day. His eye was still swollen and he was throwing up and felt generally awful. We were going to have to get him into the clinic there in Charlotte more often because he would more than likely need transfusions every other day. Justin was tired. I was tired. And things didn't seem to be getting better. I went to Facebook again and asked everyone to pray for Justin, and I asked God to help him turn some sort of corner even though there was no corner in sight. It was just a long, barren road.

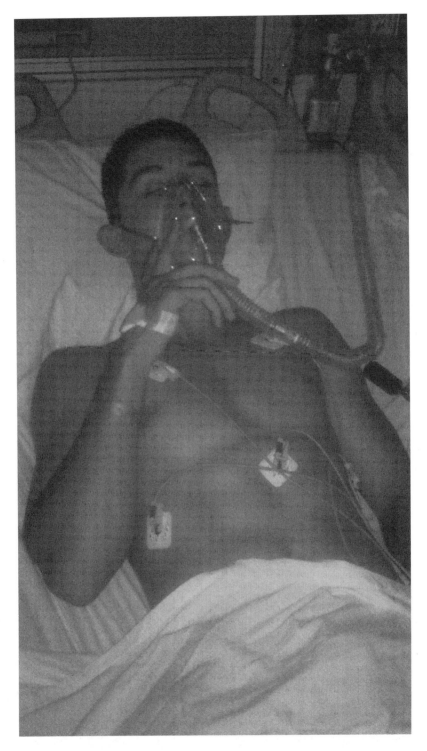

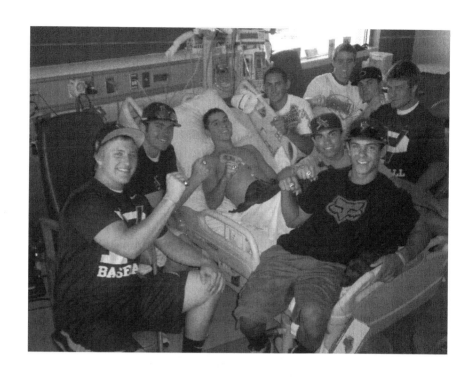

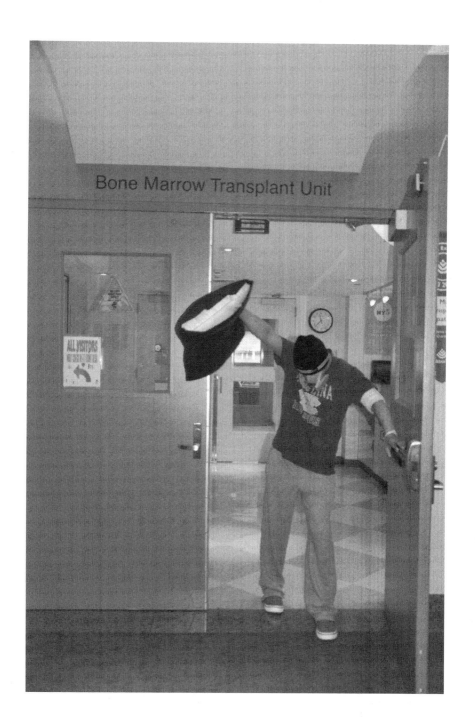

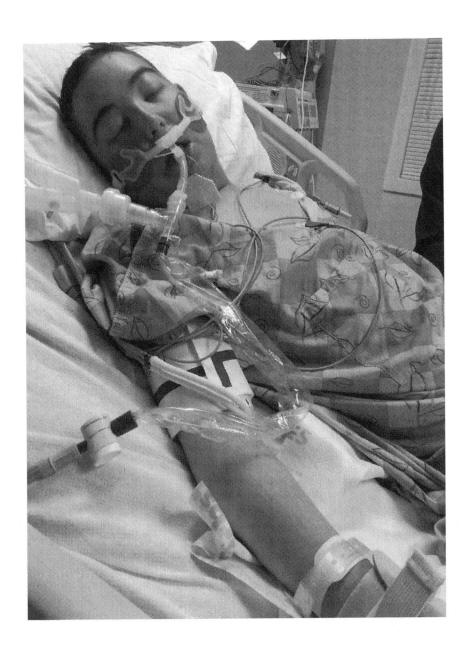

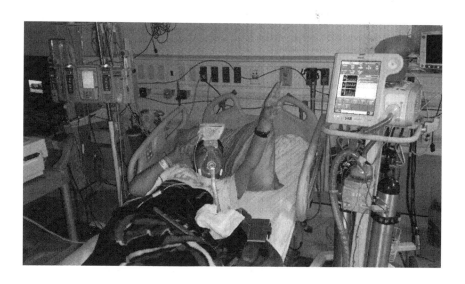

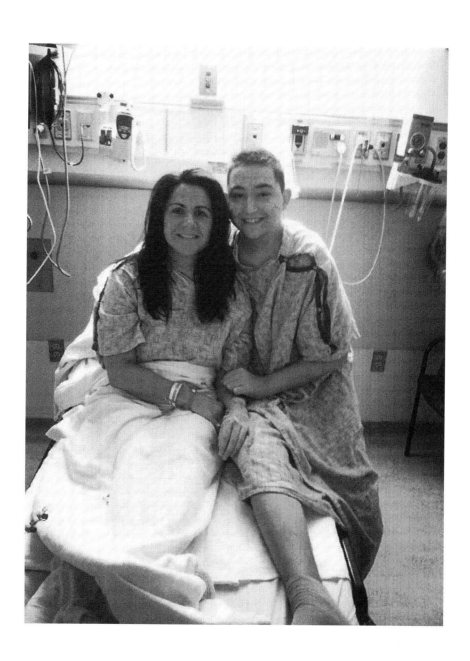

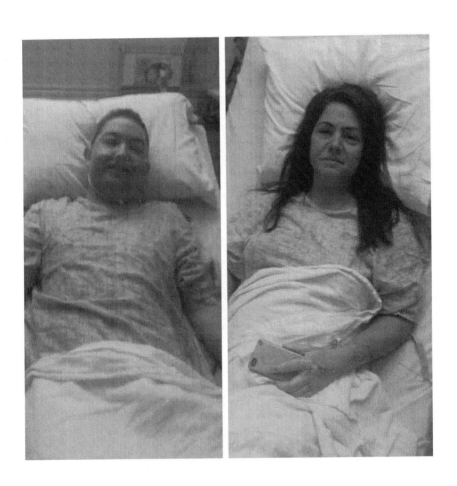

CHAPTER 22

About a week later, we were back in Durham. Justin's platelets were at 9k and his red blood was at 7.8k so he got transfusions of both. He also got Solaris in a higher dose that day. They wanted us to be at the hospital through the following Saturday and then Monday - Wednesday the next week for plasmapheresis. They decided to go ahead and get Justin back on plasmapheresis and wanted to hit the ground running. We were tired. It was a soul tired, that deep down to your core tired. Have you ever been caught outside in a cold rainstorm or when it's snowing and you stay out there much longer than you should? You stay out there so long that you freeze to your core and when you finally do go inside, you still can't get warm? That's how tired we were. Our souls were tired and there wasn't any amount of sleep that would rejuvenate us. We needed something. We needed some peace. We desperately needed Justin to catch a break. We just needed something to go our way.

Sometimes I felt like the more I begged God to help Justin, the tougher things became. Not a week later, Justin was admitted to a hospital in Charlotte with difficulty breathing. When he talked, we could hear the fluid gurgling around in his chest. Upon admittance, I told the doctors about Justin's complicated medical history and they immediately looked worried. An X-ray of his lungs showed fluid and his oxygen saturation dipped causing them to put him on oxygen. Justin wasn't doing well and we all felt more comfortable with his doctors at the Durham hospital treating him, but we were 2 hours from Durham. I called Dr. Smith right away, told him what happened and updated him on what the doctors were saying. He too wanted Justin there in Durham. He went to work on things, promising to call me back, while Justin and I waited in his room at the Charlotte hospital. Justin's oxygen saturation dropped even more and he asked for help breathing. He had on a mask that was delivering oxygen but he was still struggling. The nurses told us that they couldn't give Justin any more oxygen as he was already on the highest setting without being intubated. I felt a piece of panic settle in my chest as I realized just how serious the situation had become. There were so many doctors coming in and out of Justin's room. One doctor in particular, a pulmonologist, was coming in quite frequently. Pulmonologists are doctors who specialize in diseases with the respiratory system. Justin was getting progressively worse. The doctor told me that there was even more fluid in Justin's lungs. He said that Justin would have to be intubated and flown to Durham by Durham's Life Flight. I called my parents and Justin's father and I text his siblings. Tears clawed their way to the surface and burned my eyes with their ferocity. The doctor talked and my focus waned in and out as I looked from Justin to the doctor and back again.

From that point on everything moved at warp speed for a while. So many nurses came in to prep Justin and take him to ICU. I went to him and sat beside him on the bed. I ran my fingers through his hair and asked if he could hear me. He nodded. I asked him if he understood what was about to happen. He nodded but I told him again anyway. Then I told him I was going to pray with him. My throat ached from the knot inside it that was trying to push back tears. I tried so hard to utter a prayer without crying. I couldn't do it. I didn't want to break down in front of Justin. I didn't want him to hear the fear and worry in my voice. I couldn't do it though. I cried as I asked God to watch over him and to protect him and keep him safe. Then he was gone. They whisked him away to the ICU and the tears just came.

Jenna and my parents showed up and we were all escorted to the ICU by the nurse. We waited and waited. Finally, I went into the ICU to see if I could get any information on him. As I walked in, I saw Justin in the first room I passed, surrounded by 5 nurses. I walked in and they all just looked at me like I shouldn't have been there. I told them I was his mom and asked how he was. As I asked, one nurse moved and I could see him. I saw him lying there with a large tube down his throat. He had tears running down his cheeks and looked to be in pain. They said they were still trying to make him comfortable. That image was burned into my mind and years later I could still see him that way. When your heart breaks, do the pieces ever fully get put back together? Is it ever the same? I told him I would be back soon and gave them time to help him feel better. I went back to the waiting room and waited and waited with Jenna and my parents. We tried to formulate a plan as to how everyone would get to Durham. I was going to go with Justin if they let me. If not, I would go with Jenna and my parents would bring Jordan and his family. I went back to the ICU to see if things were better with Justin. The nurses weren't in the room with him so I went in. He had fresh tears in the corners of his closed eyes and it broke me to see my son so vulnerable. He opened his eyes and panicked. He was clearly in pain and I stepped outside his room to get a nurse. She went in the room and just told him to take deep breaths. I thought, "Really??" He looked like he wanted to punch her. I didn't understand why he was even conscious. They had him on some pain meds and one of the meds had amnesia like effects, so every time he opened his eyes, he became extremely scared and anxious because he didn't understand where he was or what was going on. It must have been so frightening for him. I couldn't imagine. He opened his eyes frequently and I hated it. I was angry. He shouldn't have been in pain like that. I told the nurse and she said that they were getting him a morphine drip. Jenna and I were back in ICU with him and my parents left and went to get Jordan's family. I called the Ronald McDonald House and made arrangements so my parents could check in there if they got there before us. Life Flight said they would get to Charlotte around 3:00 PM and that I couldn't fly with him. We decided that Jenna and I would drive to Durham after we dropped off her car at her apartment. She and I stayed with Justin, talking to him (although he couldn't talk) and rubbing his arms and his legs. He continued to be in pain though he wasn't waking up as frequently. Life Flight arrived right on time. They gave Justin a lot of meds to make him comfortable on the flight. I saw an immediate change in him. He relaxed so much. He opened his eyes at one point and motioned for a pen. He wrote down, "Cross that off my bucket list" - in reference to flying in a helicopter. They put him on a stretcher as I told him I loved him and would see him in Durham. It broke my heart to have him taken from me when he was so fragile. Then he winked at me. This kid had a rather large tube shoved down this throat but was trying to reassure me that he was going to be okay. My heart ached for him even more. Why did he have to go through all of this?

Jenna and I jumped in my car and literally sped down I-85 towards Durham. When we were about 30 minutes away, I got a phone call saying that Justin had arrived at the hospital in Durham safely and was in ICU. I hated being away from him and couldn't hurry fast enough to get to him. Jenna was always so good at keeping me calm. She just had that way about her. It was amazing. I wasn't completely calm but I was calm enough to be able to drive and that was saying something.

Jenna and I arrived and went straight to the ICU. Justin was on isolation so we had to gown up to go see him. It was agony to see him that way. He was swollen because of all the fluid in him. He was unconscious and had tubes everywhere. He looked lifeless and I was, without question, frightened. My stomach clinched as I traced my gloved fingers over his arm and talked to him. I told him he had made it safely and that he would be okay. I told him how it was necessary to intubate him to get him there so they could help him. I said so many things that I desperately wanted to be true. Jenna came in and we sat with him and talked to him, rubbing his arms. The ICU was much nicer than others he had been in. He had to share a room with someone else and that wasn't ideal but overall things were much better. My parents and Jordan's family as well as my Aunt Joan and Uncle Vic showed up shortly after we arrived. We all took turns going in to sit with Justin. I went to sit beside Jordan in the waiting room, our shoulders touching but not saying a word. We didn't speak. We just sat together feeling drawn by our common pain. Jordan loved Justin so much. They had become so close. It broke him to know what his brother was going through and not knowing when or if the unthinkable would happen.

"I was heartbroken. I couldn't believe it. I thought my little brother was going to die."-Jordan

The nurses came in regularly to move Justin around so he wouldn't get bed sores. I just stared at him as I seemed to do often still wondering how our lives led us to that place. He was getting scheduled platelet transfusions 4 times a day because his body was destroying all of his platelets. The doctors were thinking he had an infection in his lungs as opposed to hemorrhaging but weren't sure. Justin was scheduled for a bronchoscopy the next day and was given pherisis as his kidneys took a huge hit and his creatinine had climbed to 4.3 as of that morning. He was still intubated and still with amazing staff in ICU.

Everyone left on the second day that he was in ICU. I stayed with him all day, only leaving late at night to try to sleep some at the RMH and returning early the next morning. On his 4th day in ICU, Justin woke up. The days felt like weeks and so much goes on in the course of the day that I couldn't possibly remember everything. Justin had his bronchoscopy and his lungs looked bad. The doctors were thinking he had an infection of some sort and sent off fluid from his lungs for testing. In addition, he had a rash on his stomach that the doctors thought was connected to the infection in his lungs. They took two biopsies of the rash and sent them off as well. His kidneys were struggling greatly and there was discussion of dialysis. Their concern was that if they did dialysis, even once, his kidneys might shut down and he might have to have dialysis indefinitely. In the four days Justin was unconscious in ICU, they pulled about 24 pounds of fluid off of him with Lasix. They were trying to wean him off the ventilator but when they did so, he woke up in distress. He needed something but couldn't communicate what. He asked for a pen but couldn't write. I asked him to point to what was wrong and he very slowly pointed to his tube. I asked if he needed more air and he slowly nodded. They were able to take care of his request immediately. Justin had a good night. He woke up and was very alert. He wrote down questions and things he wanted to say. They eventually took out his breathing tube and he was breathing with the use of a nasal cannula. The kidney doctor said that he was doing so well that they weren't going to do dialysis at that point. We both breathed a sigh of relief. I have seen so many miracles happen with Justin. I have seen him go into remission, come through horrendous conditions, high fevers break, infections get under control, counts come into check, and then I saw him get extubated and his kidney numbers stand still. My heart was so full and I was so thankful.

Ironically, Thanksgiving was a few days later. We couldn't think of anything we were more thankful for. Justin was moved to the BMT floor days before and was making marked improvements. His lungs were clearing up. He was getting platelet transfusions twice a day and blood transfusions once every two days. They even let him go on a short pass to the Ronald McDonald House to enjoy a low-key Thanksgiving with his family. He felt awful and lay on the couch while visiting with everyone but he was there and we were all thankful for that miracle.

CHAPTER 23

I kept waiting for Justin to improve enough to be discharged. I kept waiting for him to make this miraculous turnaround and not need constant care in one form or another. I used to be that person who would always think on the positive side and I somehow believed that if I was positive enough, if I said enough times that Justin would be okay or prayed enough, that it would all turn around permanently and he would get better. But it didn't. And I didn't understand that for a long time.

We got a rather scary report the following morning from the nephrology (kidney) doctor. He asked Jason and me to step into the hall to speak with us but Justin asked that he say what he needed to in front of him. The doctor then went on to say that Justin's creatinine was the highest it had been and his kidneys were near failure. He also said that he thought we were headed in the direction of Justin needing dialysis. He felt that the damage done was permanent. I explained that Justin wouldn't need dialysis, that he just liked to keep the doctors on their toes. He was wonderful and said that Justin definitely did do that.

The next few days were a series of ups and downs. Justin was discharged from the hospital but we were asked to stay at the Ronald McDonald House close by. They talked about letting us go back to Charlotte the following Monday but it was a tough spot as Justin needed daily platelet transfusions. They even talked about starting Justin on a medication that would generate platelet production. But, not even a day after he was discharged we were back at the hospital in Durham and Justin's kidneys were worse. They were calling in the nephrology team again to get their take on Justin. The doctors decided to continue to monitor Justin's kidneys outpatient. They didn't understand how he was still peeing, with only 10% kidney function. We were beginning December and it was glaringly apparent that Justin had been in the hospital more than he had been out of it that year. We were going into the hospital just about daily. He was still getting antibiotics and antifungals.

If it wasn't one thing, it was definitely another: high blood pressure, antibiotics, severe headaches, high potassium, low potassium, platelet transfusions, blood transfusions, increases in BUN (Blood Urea Nitrogen – used to determine how well the kidneys are working by measuring the amount of urea nitrogen in the blood) and creatinine, Nplate injections to increase platelet production and the list goes on. "Nplate works with the cells in the bone marrow to make more platelets by helping increase platelet production, which can help increase the number of healthy platelets in your body. Nplate does this by imitating TPO, the protein that helps cells in the bone marrow to make more platelets."[13] Over time, it actually started to work for Justin. As it always seemed to go with Justin, when we saw an improvement in one area, some other area suffered. It was that balancing act again. Justin was finally able to go home to Charlotte for the weekend and we both just fell into the couch, soaking up every ounce of normalcy that we could. But on the following Monday we were back in Durham and his kidney numbers were the highest they had ever been. The nephrologist came in to talk to us. He explained that unless there was a miracle, Justin would need a kidney transplant. Dr. Reynolds said that he would have to be on dialysis for quite some time before getting a transplant because they wanted him stable and wanted to be sure that his cancer didn't return. They were right on the verge of starting Justin on dialysis but wanted to wait until absolutely necessary. We talked briefly about using my kidney for Justin's transplant if it came to that and then I turned to Justin and asked him what he thought. He responded calmly and simply, "I will do whatever God wants me to do. I say that to Him when I pray. I tell him, "God, I will do whatever you want me to do - just please try to make it a little easier." Justin continued to blow me away day in and day out. His faith was increasing with every single trial, and there were plenty. I knew, as I do now, that Justin has a divine purpose.

Two days later Justin was admitted back to the hospital in Durham. His kidneys were in failure and only functioning at about 10%. He had put on 14 pounds of fluid. They wanted to try to pull that fluid off so he didn't go into respiratory failure again. They were able to pull off a significant amount of fluid and let him go home two days later. He was on a fluid restriction but he was happy to be home. So, with this fluid restriction - can you imagine only being allowed a few tablespoons of water every hour? Sometimes Justin would save his tablespoons so the next hour or by the end of the day he could have a significant amount to drink. He was so thirsty. He just wanted to be able to drink water. He wasn't being greedy. He didn't crave Gatorade or tea or soda, just water. And don't we all know how good water is for us, that we should drink at least half of our body weight in ounces every day? But he couldn't. His life depended on him *not* drinking fluid. Some days you could surely find me with my head in my hands wondering how in the world any of this was real.

A couple of days before Christmas that year, Justin was diagnosed with parainfluenza 3, and five days after that he was admitted to the hospital in Durham with pneumonia. He had fought so hard against the need for dialysis but I guess God had a different plan for him. If it was a matter of dialysis a few times to give his kidneys a rest, we would have already done that. However, the likelihood of Justin's kidneys completely stopping once they began dialysis were very high. I just didn't want that to be one more thing. Another challenge on top of everything he'd had to deal with.

You sometimes want your life, or at least an event in your life, to be like one in the movies. You know, where everything is going wrong but then there is this one moment, this defining moment that just changes everything and turns everything around for the better. You not only wait for it but you bust your butt to make it happen and you actively expect that it will. At least I did. Justin was moved to the ICU. The bottom of his lungs started to collapse and he just could not catch his breath. He couldn't get a deep enough breath and would sit up in bed and reach for air with everything he had. They moved him to ICU and put him on BiPAP to help keep his lungs open and give him the air he needed. BiPAP stands for "Bilevel Positive Airway Pressure and it is a form of non-invasive mechanical pressure support ventilation that uses a time-cycled or flow-cycled change between two different applied levels of positive airway pressure."[14] I cannot wait to see the plans that God has for Justin in this life. I know that His plans are far better than anything I could have ever planned for him. Everything in His time. I know that but when it's your child you just want him to be okay - now.

As Justin struggled to breathe in the ICU with the doctors and nurses moving busily around him, I watched him search the room. I asked him what he was looking for and he asked if Dr. Smith was there. Dr. Smith had always given Justin such peace. He is a brilliant man and also compassionate. Justin felt such security when he was around. It was 2:00 AM when Justin asked for his doctor. Dr. Smith wasn't on call. He didn't have to be there, but when the hospital called him to tell him that his patient was being moved to ICU, he came in immediately. When Justin asked for him I said, "He's right here." Dr. Smith walked over to him so Justin could see him and told Justin that they were going to make him feel better soon. The BiPAP machine was helping him breathe and they were starting him on dialysis for the first time. I fought hard for Justin to not need dialysis. We did everything we could, everything we knew to do. And because we did everything and he still ended up needing it, we knew it was God's plan. Dialysis wasn't an option anymore, it was necessary.

114

A couple of days after being moved to ICU, Justin was moved back to the BMT floor. He remained on the BiPAP machine with quite a bit of oxygen and they continued dialysis. On New Year's Eve, Justin was finally able to come off the BiPAP machine; however, he continued receiving dialysis. He usually felt terrible after dialysis. He was always fatigued and would usually get even more nauseated. He took a nap after his New Year's Eve session and was feeling well enough later in the evening to order his meal of choice, Chinese, and welcome in the New Year with a positive attitude and an overwhelming sense of hope for 2013.

"I feel like we didn't know the deepest corners of true emotion or the rawest parts of ourselves until Justin got sick. We were all living an average life and didn't appreciate the highs or lows like we should have. Worrying about things like work or what to make for dinner or dirty laundry no longer mattered. In a sense, this journey woke us up and made us appreciate life. It truly made us love harder and live bolder." –Jenna

Justin was finally discharged about a week later. We set him up with outpatient dialysis in Charlotte 3 times a week and continued weekly visits to Durham. He struggled a lot with dialysis and, after doing some research, I asked his nephrologist at the hospital about peritoneal dialysis. It would allow him to do the dialysis at home at night while he slept. He was very tired of hospitals. He simply didn't want to be in them anymore than he absolutely had to be. We thought that having dialysis at home every night would help. It did require another catheter - this one in his stomach. The doctors talked about a probable kidney transplant. I think they were tired of me telling them that there was still a chance that Justin would be able to come off dialysis altogether and that his kidneys could heal. He was still peeing, though very little. They were still trying to determine what happened to his kidneys. They were thinking he had Atypical HUS but they couldn't trace it back to how or why he would have gotten that. None of the treatments for that worked. They put him back on Solaris, this time for a longer period of time, with the hopes that it would do the trick. They didn't know what they would try if it didn't work and they said that they needed to know, and have a handle on, what caused his kidneys to fail so that the same thing wouldn't happen to his transplanted kidney. It all seemed so twisted. Nothing made much sense to anyone and it was sure easy to start to get discouraged.

January 20th was Justin's 1 year anniversary for his bone marrow transplant. He was feeling well and wasn't in the hospital so I seized the opportunity to take him, his brother and his sister up to Boone, North Carolina to go snowboarding at Sugar Mountain. Justin hadn't been snowboarding in a couple of years and then there was the issue of neuropathy in his feet and also balance issues. But he was alive and he was smiling and we decided to live in those moments and soak up as much life as we could. He actually did quite well, considering. He sat down near the bottom of the hill and I helped him strap into his snowboard and then helped him stand up. I stood just below him and held his hands as he tried to remember what it felt like to be on a board. The first few tries were tough as he was understandably unsteady and uncertain. By the end of the day, however, he improved significantly and couldn't wait to go back.

Justin settled into a routine of the hospital in Durham every Monday for infusions and count checks and then dialysis in Charlotte on Tuesdays, Thursdays and Saturdays. Some days they would take off as much as 10 pounds of fluid. I just couldn't imagine what that was doing to his poor body. His counts all remained relatively the same and the doctors continued to look for different things that would address his Atypical HUS and treat it so he would be transplant ready the following year, if need be. He felt decent on his in between days. His vision was still about half of what it should have been and that was frustrating as he couldn't play video games and even watching TV was hard. He still had neuropathy in his feet (trauma to his nerves that resulted in numbness). It was such a miracle and a blessing to see him out and active given all of the complications that he continued to deal with, but that was Justin. He had this attitude of resilience. That's not to say that he didn't struggle. He still struggled plenty but overall he made the most of every day and still managed to keep me laughing.

By the end of that January we met with the peritoneal dialysis folks to further discuss that kind of dialysis as an option for Justin. He was sure that he wanted to go forward with it so we scheduled a time for surgery to place the catheter in his stomach. They also suggested that we go ahead and put Justin on the donor list. Even though I was determined to be his donor, we still had to put him on the list and then apply to use a living donor. This made my stomach hurt as we just kept praying his kidneys would heal, to somehow salvage and utilize what he had left anyway, and he wouldn't need a transplant. Of course, we would do whatever we had to for him. But just over a week later, Justin went in for dialysis and they declared him End Stage Renal Disease, which is the complete, or near complete, failure of the kidneys. On top of that, his creatinine jumped to 7.2 and his BUN was high. We weren't giving up on complete healing. The day before Justin was on the slopes again. He took it easy but amazed me nonetheless. There were a few times he was just whizzing down the slope and my heart was so full, as were my eyes with tears. When we finished for the day, he looked at me and said, "You know what mom...those last 3 runs, as I was coming down...I didn't even feel sick." My heart ached and soared at the same time. Because that's what it's all about, isn't it? Finding that peace and that feeling of health and healing in the midst of uncertainty and pain. He found it on the slope with the wind humming by him and the fresh air filling his lungs.

CHAPTER 24

When Justin received his bone marrow transplant, it was from an unrelated donor. We were told that we couldn't meet this person for at least a year post-transplant. All they would tell us was that she was a woman in her 30's. Our mind spun and all we wanted was to know who she was. We wanted to know who was saving Justin's life. We wrote her letters within that year and sent her a gift but had no idea who she was. At the end of February 2013 we found out who Justin's angel was - Jessica Johnson from Florida. I'll never forget how Justin stared at the piece of paper with her name, address and phone number on it on our way home from Durham that day. Justin gripped it in one hand and his phone in the other working up the nerve to call her. What do you say to the person who saved your life? Finally, Justin deliberately and slowly pressed her phone number into his phone. The next thing I heard was, "Hi, my name is Justin Solomon and I think you saved my life." We talked to Jessica, in one form or another, every day. She started planning a trip to meet us so we were very excited for that. I was nervous and excited at the same time. I was going to meet the person who so unselfishly gave of herself and saved my son's life. How do you even go about thanking someone for that? It isn't like she bought us a blender. She gave my son a second chance and in doing so, did the same for me too.

"The Marrow Program required a 1 year gap between donating and eligibility to contact my recipient. I spent hours trying to find this person in the beginning, but finally gave up due to frustration. Fran called one day and said there was a package delivered to her office for me. I intentionally waited until my mother came home so we could open it together. She was such a great support system, I thought it would be nice to open it together. There were 3 letters and a Pandora bracelet with a guardian angel charm. We read the letters and cried, knowing we had done something great, something amazing.

I was asked to do an on camera interview to promote the Be The One run in Tampa. The interview was great and I mentioned how excited I was for the opportunity to meet my recipient. Two days later my phone rang and this nice young man on the other line introduced himself. He said, "Hello, my name is Justin Solomon and I think you saved my life." Sometimes people have an "ah-ha moment" and this was mine. All the days and nights I thought about him, hoping and praying he was doing well, wanting to hear his voice and here he is... with his amazing mother Jennifer, on the phone. I spent 6 hours talking to Jennifer that evening. I told her my story and the adventure it was to get where we are, wanting so bad to meet in person.

March 9, 2013 I walked into Hendrick Motorsports complex in Charlotte, NC for what would be one of the best days of my life. The plan was for me to stay with Jennifer and Justin in their Charlotte home for the weekend. The press was there and I was nervous and excited all at the same time. I kept my cool until the doors opened and there were my angels, Jennifer and Justin. I had waited over a year for this perfect day and it was just that, perfect. We gave individual interviews after our meeting and I remember saying, "I feel like I'm the lucky one."

Bone marrow donation changed my life in so many amazing ways. When I think about all of things I've done in my life there is nothing that makes me happier and more appreciated. The Solomon family is a close knit, complex, and selfless family that has experienced tremendous hardship during Justin's illness. I feel privileged to know such a wonderful family and I'm confident our relationship will never end. I'm so thankful to my surgery day angel, my mother who was there for my recovery, and my father for always encouraging me to do the right thing."—Jessica

We didn't have to wait long to meet Jessica. Within a couple of weeks we were scheduled to meet her in Charlotte. The Hendrick Marrow Foundation asked to host the meeting at the Charlotte Speedway and filmed everything. We were a little worried the day before as Justin had some fluid in his lungs again and we were concerned that we would have to go back to the hospital. By the next day, Justin seemed better. The fluid seemed to be working itself out of his lungs. He knew his body so well by that point and knew every time he was headed into respiratory failure but he felt better and we had a date with his donor that day.

We were in an open room with a lot of people from the Be the Match Foundation and our family of course. I was shaking and I think Justin was too. And then Jessica walked in and was as beautiful as she was kind. We embraced for a very long time. I cried, of course. We said these words that we somehow tried to tie our deepest feelings to - "Thank you." We all told her thank you and as we did, I came to realize how stupid it sounded. "Thank you" wasn't what I meant, it wasn't what I felt. What I felt wasn't just in the deepest parts of my guts - it coursed through my body. It resided in my heart and ran through my blood. It flooded my head and spilled from my eyes. It was everything I was. Thank you couldn't describe what I was feeling but it was all I had and so I gave it freely.

Jessica was hope incarnate for us.

Justin was admitted to a hospital in Charlotte the following day for an infection. The doctors started him on antibiotics in the middle of the night and he began feeling much better. They weren't sure what was going on with him but they thought it was a viral or bacterial infection in his blood. They did a chest X-ray and a CT scan that night and saw that he had pneumonia. It was his left lung that was affected this time, where usually it was in his right lung. They only kept him overnight since he was scheduled to go to Durham the next day. About 10 days later, we were back in Durham for Justin's normal Monday visit. He still had pneumonia and his platelets were still down somewhat because of him getting sick. We found out that Justin could potentially have his kidney transplant as soon as September that year. That news caused a mixture of emotions. We felt excitement because the sooner we could get him back to "normal" the better. He hated dialysis and it always made him feel terrible. We also had feelings of stress and anxiety over another transplant and all of the things that could potentially be difficult or go wrong. If we all remember, Justin liked to keep things interesting. He couldn't do anything the easy way or the way that anyone else did it. He had to be unique. He used to joke around that he was just trying to help the doctors figure things out before other people ended up needing the same things. One of the things that had to be figured out before he could have the kidney transplant was his lungs. They were so weak and parts of them continued to collapse and he continued to get pneumonia. There was also the issue of Atypical HUS. That part was still so confusing and could also affect if Justin was able to get a transplant at all. We, of course, turned to prayer. We asked for prayers for complete healing but also for guidance. We weren't sure where to go or how to even attempt getting there.

Amidst the doctor's appointments, dialysis, medication and so forth as I mentioned before - life still happened. There were still birthdays, celebrations, illnesses, heartbreak, rejoicing, moving, etc. Life still happened all around us. Justin's life seemed to have slowed to a crawl, almost completely stopping a few times. But life didn't wait for us to catch up. It just kept right on going. Maybe this is a good place for me to apologize - mostly to my older 2 kids, Jordan and Jenna:

I know I got tunnel vision when Justin got sick. I know it became who I was to get him better. I know you two were older and already doing your thing but I also know that you always need your mom. I'm so sorry that I wasn't there as much, that we didn't talk as much. I can tell you that I did love you as much. I did the best I could and I do understand that maybe it wasn't always good enough. You were both so loving and supportive of your brother. You both came to visit him no matter where he was and you called and text him regularly. I'm so deeply thankful for your sibling bond. Just please know that your mom always loved you deeper and farther.

We went about Justin's normal day to day which nearly every day included a hospital in one form or another. Justin was still going in for hemodialysis and it continued to kick his ass. This day was particularly hard on Justin as it was painful and scary. The nurses messed up and left him on the dialysis machine longer than he should have been. I asked them repeatedly if they had added time to his session. He was going longer because he came in with more fluid after the longer weekend and we expected that. He was supposed to be dialyzed for 4 hours but just after the 4 hour mark, I saw that he still had 50 minutes to go. He had been cramping badly and I was hoping to get him off the machine quickly. I asked one nurse if they added more time. She said no and I asked another. The second nurse was snippy and I explained that if he was, in fact, supposed to only be dialyzed for 4 hours, he should have been done by then. She finally looked into it and realized I was right. Right about then Justin went white as a sheet and fell back in his chair. He was rolling his head from side to side and mumbling that he felt "funny." He started reaching for my hand and I was trying to talk to him to keep him awake but he was going in and out. His blood pressure dropped. The nurse kept saying that she was going to give him some blood back and he would feel better. Then I saw that his tube was black, where usually it was red with his blood. I asked the nurse why it was black and she said he had a clot. She disconnected him immediately and he laid back and just rested for a while. So many things that scared me happened nearly every day with him. Dialysis was so hard on his body. He was getting hemodialysis 3 times a week and on those days, he was completely drained. He would come home and lay either in bed or on the couch for the rest of the day. On his off days, he tried to do a little more but it wasn't much. We would be able to start him on peritoneal dialysis at home within the next week so we were hoping that would be easier on him.

I had to go through weeks and weeks of training in order to give Justin home dialysis. It was the first time I had ever been thankful for so much training; as a former teacher, I was never a fan of trainings. We were finally given the green light and Justin and I were both excited to see if home dialysis was any easier on him. I soon felt like I was a business owner, placing orders, receiving deliveries, making calculations. It was all so surreal.

Justin slept with me a lot so I could monitor him. They left the double lumen Vas-Cath in his chest in case he ever needed emergency hemodialysis again. Every night I used the tube in his stomach to hook him up to the dialysis machine. Depending on how much fluid Justin had in a day, we determined what strength of dextrose to use. The dialysate absorbed the waste products in the stomach lining and then was drawn back out of his body and discarded into a waste bag. It ran for 8 hours. How he slept I'll never know. I guess sometimes he didn't. The cramping continued off and on. I would rub his hands or his calves when the pain would sit him upright in bed. We googled everything on how to ease the cramping and why it was happening, in addition to asking the doctors, of course. But Justin's cramping was different and even when they gave him supplements to balance his electrolytes, he still cramped. We tried everything, including tablespoons of mustard. Sometimes we would think it worked only to realize on a different occasion, it didn't. We pulled off 8-10 pounds of fluid frequently but he still had more to take. For some reason it seemed to be taking off less and less. We were at the Durham hospital about a week later and they wanted to admit him for a few days to try to get him back in check. He was up about 13 pounds in fluid and with his creatinine at 11, the doctors had numerous concerns. We opted out of having him admitted and went for option two which was to go back to Durham for a long session of hemodialysis the following day. We were hoping that would help get him back to a safe place. Justin was worried because he hated hemodialysis and didn't want to have to go back to that every other day. In addition, we were all very concerned about his fluid overload because of his lungs. Upon further inspection, the doctors realized that the tube in Justin's stomach had sucked up against the lining and wasn't able to pull as much off so they had to operate again to fix it. Justin's surgery was scheduled for the next day as he needed to have a dialysis session to get some of that fluid off. He was in pain from the tube moving so we were all hoping they could get him in quickly. Because of the incisions in his stomach, he would have to have hemodialysis for the rest of the week and the following week also. Justin was in some pain after the surgery but did okay with the week of hemodialysis and was happy to get back on peritoneal dialysis at home.

A couple of weeks later we set out to embark on yet another phase of his journey. Justin had blood taken while at the Durham hospital for tissue typing to begin the process of his kidney transplant. I have to tell you the range of emotions that came over me as his doctor came in and told us he wanted to do that. Of course, Justin was so ready to get on with it, get on with his life and have the kidney transplant but it sent me for a tailspin. I went back in time to his HLA typing for his bone marrow transplant. It seemed like we went into that so blind. We had no idea what lay after that and then seeing all of the complications and where it led us, to him needing a kidney, I had to wonder if we made the right decisions or if the decisions were even ours to make. You think about everything and you *overthink*. There was no easy answer and no easy solution. Justin was, for the most part, doing okay even though things were up and down all the time. He was in pain, his life was not his own, he was at risk for respiratory distress, among other things, but on the other hand he was there - he was alive. I got to see him every single day and listen to him breathe going to sleep every single night. I watched him enjoy many aspects of his life, although I know he felt so limited. Going into another transplant was opening up so many vulnerabilities - taking risks that we may not even have realized and the unknown was absolutely terrifying. I had to make myself breathe that day as we went through with the testing and as I thought about everything. I went over the previous two years in my head and I had a few panic attacks that day worrying about what was ahead. If I'd learned anything those past two years it was to love harder, live bolder and have faith that it would all work out. God was in control.

More than anything I wanted to be Justin's kidney donor. When he was diagnosed with cancer, I felt extremely helpless. My son was so sick, sicker than he had ever been and there was nothing I could do to help him. When we were told he would need a bone marrow transplant, I hoped and prayed that I could donate my marrow but I was only a half match. Then, I felt some hope that I would be able to donate my kidney to him. That was my goal. That was my focus. Two days after Justin's testing, I was called to go into the hospital in Durham for testing to see if I would be able to donate. The entire process would take a while and a good part of that was getting Justin to a healthy point. A transplant of any kind would take a toll on the body so Justin needed to be healthy for a period of time before his kidney transplant. That was going to be tricky.

A couple of weeks after Justin and my testing, he was admitted to the hospital in Durham because his potassium skyrocketed to 6.5. Normal is 3.5-5.0. "Your body needs a delicate balance of potassium to help the heart and other muscles work properly. But too much potassium in your blood can lead to dangerous, and possibly deadly, changes in heart rhythm."[15] They hooked him up to an EKG. In addition, his BUN was dangerously high and his creatinine was 11.1. He had to have hemodialysis for two days to try to get him straightened out. We were praying that the doctors would get him straightened out because we had a trip planned to go to New York City to meet some new friends and go to a Yankees game. We were still living in the moments in between. We knew that tough times lurked in the distance but we didn't let that rob us of our todays.

About a week after the trip, I got a phone call from the transplant coordinator in Durham concerning the typing I'd done a week or two previously. She said that my blood type was 0-, but with organ transplant they don't care about the + or -. So I'm universal and that was great. Also, when they mixed our blood together, Justin's didn't react - again, that was great news! Thirdly, they tested his and my antigens to see if any matched up. In organ transplantation there doesn't have to be matching antigens but they always like it when there are. Here's where it got tricky. Because Justin had his bone marrow transplant, his antigens had completely changed. When they did HLA typing for his bone marrow transplant, I was a half match (3/6) - normal for a parent. Justin's BMT changed his antigens entirely to that of his donor's. So they were profoundly happy when they saw that I still matched Justin 3/6. They were surprised but pleased to see it. It all seemed like a miracle to me. God was there and working feverishly in our lives. We weren't in the clear yet, not by a long shot. There were still so many things that had to happen before Justin would even be cleared for transplant. His levels were all over the place and above all he had to be healthy and strong before they would move forward with the kidney transplant. They watched his labs closely. One number they were paying attention to was his LDH (normal is around 105-250). Justin's LDH used to be above 1,000 but since starting on Solaris in January, it was stable between 450-550. We desperately needed that number to come down. The nephrologist in Durham was talking to us like he just couldn't see the transplant happening at all. At that point, I decided to look elsewhere to get a second opinion.

We continued to keep ourselves busy and decided to go up to Boone, North Carolina (where I grew up) for a friend's high school graduation. While there, Justin nearly passed out (again) and after being seen by paramedics was taken to and admitted to a hospital in Boone. We started to make jokes about Justin trying to visit the hospital or urgent care in every town we visited. It was becoming a regular thing and was almost ridiculous. It seemed as though our "living in the moments in between" was becoming harder and harder to do. Justin was in need of emergency hemodialysis as well as a blood transfusion. His Vas-Cath wasn't working properly but they discharged him with the assurance that we would have him in Durham the following day. We did get him to the hospital in Durham where he received what he needed, including a blood transfusion. His platelets were dropping quickly too and were at 60k. It seemed as though his marrow just wasn't able to produce cells like it was supposed to. Everyone was racking their brains trying to figure out what was going on inside Justin's body and why.

About a week later, we were back at Durham hospital. Justin had transplant testing all that morning and then we met with the transplant surgeon, financial advisor and nurse practitioner regarding Justin's possible kidney transplant. We were a little overwhelmed with all of the information. Afterwards we met with Justin's nephrologist, the dietician and the social worker. We had a lot to think about but all of it was moving us forward. We were thankful to be moving in that direction. We were also scared and nervous and praying for God to guide the doctors and us as we started down a new path. Justin's counts continued to make us uneasy. His red blood was still low at 7.9. They were trying to avoid a transfusion because of the antibodies. He was also having those blood pressure issues. It would bottom out and then come back up. Justin kept feeling as though he would pass out and the only thing that helped was lying down until he felt better. There was still so much that needed to be figured out. Sometimes that light at the end of the tunnel was hard to see. I figured there must be a turn in the road and maybe that's why we couldn't see it but to be honest, sometimes I wondered if there was a light at all.

CHAPTER 25

Justin was cleared to go home to New Mexico for a quick trip at the end of June. Getting to New Mexico was rough. The airline lost his luggage which included medication and items needed for dialysis. I had a bit of a freak out moment as I knew that Justin needed those things for his treatment and I worried he would go into respiratory failure with too much fluid buildup. I frantically called a doctor in Farmington who made a real effort to take care of Justin, Dr. Jacobs. He directed us to some possible options and with the help of some family and friends in Farmington, we got the supplies that Justin would need for two days until we could get his luggage back. We made the 3 hour drive to Farmington and the airline brought Justin's medical supplies to us around midnight. When medical supplies are involved, the airlines step up their game a bit. Justin was having a great visit with his friends and family and a couple of days into it, I decided that I needed to check his labs because his blood pressure had been all over the place and he was sleeping more. Dr. Rice's office was great to help when needed with Justin. Even though they weren't pediatric oncologists they still agreed to see Justin for labs. Dr. Rice ran Justin's labs and his red blood was 7.6, requiring a transfusion. His platelets were 47k, also requiring a transfusion but Justin's doctor only wanted to give him one unit of red blood because he so easily got overloaded with fluid. They didn't even want to do that but they had to. It was very frustrating because Justin had been receiving shots to increase red blood cell and platelet production and it just wasn't working. It seemed like his marrow had taken a turn and wasn't producing again.

We stayed in New Mexico for a week as Justin couldn't be away from his doctors in North Carolina for too long. It was just enough time for Justin to get his friends and family fix. After getting back to North Carolina, Justin had to get into the hospital in Durham immediately. He had a lot of funky things going on. He was admitted in quite a bit of pain all over his body and running a fever. They ran blood cultures and started him on some strong antibiotics as per protocol. By the next day he was feeling better so they released him to go back to Charlotte knowing we would be back the following Monday. His platelets were low and he was dealing with a blood blister and a bloody nose that lasted for several hours. On Monday, Justin's platelets were 30k (should be at least 150k.) but they didn't transfuse. They increased his dose of Nplate to try to give his marrow a boost in producing platelets. His red blood was 9 so no blood transfusion was needed. They did the FISH test to be sure that Justin was still all donor cells but we knew we wouldn't have results for a day or two. They scheduled a bone marrow biopsy for 2 weeks out as they wanted to see if his marrow still had low cellularity. "Cellularity refers to the percentage of cells growing in the bone marrow. Cellularity starts at 100% at birth and decreases with age."[16] There was more discussion of possibly having to go back to the donor for more cells. Justin had an EKG and an ECHO that day as well as part of his kidney transplant prep to be sure his heart was strong enough for transplant. He was nothing *but* heart so I was sure that part would be fine. We met with the cardiologist after the EKG and ECHO. He said that Justin's heart was functioning in the low-to-normal range. He didn't feel that it would be a problem during transplant but he said he just couldn't know for sure. If Justin's nephrologist wanted, they could admit Justin to the hospital 3-5 days before transplant and put him in ICU to start him on a couple of meds that would strengthen his heart. We would have to wait to hear what Justin's nephrologist wanted to do.

There was an endless amount of information to process and I found that when I was actively working on solutions or doing research, I was better able to handle things. Justin was just a mess though. He was all over the place with no rhyme or reason. Even the doctors were at a loss to so many of Justin's issues. I had to push the feelings about the situation aside and focus on the task at hand. They caught up to me though, in the oddest of places and often when I wasn't expecting them to completely overcome me. I could be at the grocery store or on a walk and I would break, with no warning. Tears shot from my eyes, my stomach clinched and my hand involuntarily shot up to cover my mouth trying to muffle the sobs and screams that would follow. Somewhere in my head I was aware that I was breaking because I tried to look as inconspicuous as possible. Crouched down, I turned my back to onlookers and my body shook as I sobbed. Even though I was aware, I couldn't control it. I couldn't stop it any more than I could have prevented it from beginning. It was a crashing wave that I had to ride out. Sometimes it felt like I was drowning under its weight. It was tremendously heavy and all consuming. But I always found my way to the surface. I always found my next breath.

I remember when my kids were small, I would check on them as they were sleeping and sometimes actually wake them up to be sure they were breathing. I did that with Justin. Sometimes he slept so quietly that I would reach over and be sure I could feel the rise and fall of his chest beneath my hand. There were times when, as I was leaning over to check on him, he would say, "I'm okay, mom."

It got to where every pain was investigated and I asked him a million questions to determine if we needed to head to the nearest hospital. It was crazy how much it varied. Some things that seemed like nothing were great big things and some things that seemed like a big deal, weren't. I felt like we were caught in a forever whirlwind, always trying to figure out his body and what it was doing. That night we were up in the middle of the night investigating leg pain that he was having. He tried hard not to wake me but I slept so light that I always knew when he was sitting on the side of the bed in pain. After an inventory of aches, pains, blood pressure, and other vitals, I researched the possibilities and as his pain eased, so did my mind somewhat. I wondered if we would ever really sleep again. If there would ever come a time when we could lay our head down and rest without worry.

On July 12th, 2013 I found out that I would be a Mimi again. Jordan, my oldest, was expecting another baby due in December. I'd discovered that I deeply loved being a Mimi. Being with Tripp was one of my very favorite things in the entire world. To know that I was going to be Mimi for a second time made me feel pretty lucky, despite the daily pain we were going through. We learned to appreciate everything back then. We discovered just how precious time and family really were.

Justin had a lot of nausea and we weren't sure why. He always had nausea but he had it even more lately. We were scheduled to go back to Durham on the following Monday for infusions, a bone marrow biopsy and a psychological evaluation. The psych evaluation was part of his pre-transplant evaluation. I was called to go back in and continue my medical evaluation as Justin's potential donor as well. I was scheduled to go in for two days a week for the following two weeks as part of my medical evaluation. Justin would more than likely be presented before the committee the first week of August to determine if he was ready for transplant. And if I passed all the testing, they would present me to the committee the following week. The committee consisted of all of Justin's current doctors as well as the surgeons who would perform the kidney transplant. They were meeting to discuss a timetable for the transplant. It was a nervous but exciting time and I know that Justin was so ready for that break to come.

Exactly two years from the day we were told he had cancer, Justin was back in the hospital in Durham. We didn't expect that he would still be struggling the way he was with so many complications. We definitely never expected that we would be awaiting the go ahead for a kidney transplant. I recalled when he had his bone marrow transplant and we thought that was going to be the worst of it. We thought that he was on his way to health and happiness. Isn't life exactly what you never expected?!? God was steering this crazy boat we were in and we were doing our best to just enjoy the ride and be thankful for the moments we had, the friends we encountered and the memories we made along the way. We weren't in the business of giving up. There was just too much to live for and we knew that Justin's break was on the horizon.

Not long after those appointments, I received a packet in the mail from the hospital in Durham saying that I had been found to be COMPATIBLE with Justin but they had to be sure I was healthy enough to donate my kidney so there was still a mountain of testing I had to undergo. Knowing that would be the case, I had already started a workout and diet regimen so the doctors couldn't possibly find a reason to say no. God helps those who help themselves. That was me doing my part by helping myself and I was just praying that the doctors would find me in complete good health so that I could donate my kidney to my son. It felt like things were coming together.

A few days later, Justin had labs at the clinic in Charlotte. Most of his counts were stable, out of whack as usual but stable. But one in particular was steadily rising and it was a very, very bad sign. Justin had been going to Durham every two weeks to receive that infusion of Solaris to try to keep him in a stable place and keep his ATypical HUS at bay. That had been working fairly well and his LDH, while not normal, had been stable between 450 and 550. Testing had not shown any schistocytes (broken red blood cells) that would indicate active HUS (the condition for which they had been treating Justin). We just weren't sure what was going on with him. We weren't sure why his LDH was steadily rising again and now at 722.

CHAPTER 26

For once it was me off to Durham while Justin stayed home. I headed north for my first round of testing to potentially be Justin's kidney donor. It was a full day that lasted from 7:30 AM – 4:00 PM. I had labs first thing in the morning and then I talked with the transplant coordinator, nephrologists, psychologist, and social worker. Lastly, I had an EKG and an ultrasound. Things were still very early but they seemed to start off on a good note. The following day I was off again. First was a long test that would test my kidney function and a chest X-ray.

I was nervous but also strangely confident. I wanted to be Justin's donor more than I'd wanted anything in quite a while. I'd always been relatively healthy and I just couldn't imagine not being able to do that for him. Of course, I couldn't affect the matching or blood type. I had no control over that. On that part, I put my faith and trust in God. The following day I got some results back from the testing. The chest X-ray looked great. With the kidney function study, they wanted the results to be 80% or better. My kidneys were functioning at 92.4%. We were hopeful.

A few days later Justin was struggling with bone pain and muscle cramping. He had trouble walking and, of course, the ever present nausea. His sleeping was often interrupted with pain. He was napping on one occasion and I walked into the room. I saw his hands trembling but he was so tired that he was able to sleep through it. I lay down beside him and slipped my hand into his to try to steady him. Tears escaped from the corners of my eyes as I wondered, "When was enough, enough?" When would it stop? When would God say, "Okay, you've done your time and you did well." I don't mean that I wanted Justin to be granted the ultimate rest. God knows I didn't want that. I simply wanted him to walk and not grow tired, to eat without the worry of nausea, to sleep without trembling. Just some normalcy, that's all I wanted for him.

Several days after that were emotionally charged days at the hospital. Justin had appointments in the morning and I had another test in the afternoon. Justin's labs were relatively stable. Again, they weren't normal by any stretch but stable. We talked with his doctor because they were scheduled to present Justin to the committee on August 22nd. Justin asked his bone marrow transplant doctor, Dr. Smith, if he was still going to give his approval for this kidney transplant, given his recent issues. His doctor said absolutely and that he had already attended one meeting and sent several emails on the subject. I was somewhat surprised but I trusted his doctor completely and I trusted God even more.

As I mentioned, from the time we found out that Justin would need a kidney transplant, I desperately wanted to be the one to donate my kidney to him. I prayed that somehow, someway I would be a match - that I would be found medically sound and that the process would go smoothly (because nothing had gone smoothly for Justin). I was astounded at how smoothly everything progressed. From the minute I turned in my paperwork; everything had been so easy, every test came back with positive results and every meeting had been informative and helpful. I had my last test and my last meeting. They did a CT scan to get a good look at my kidneys and to determine which kidney they would take. I met with the transplant surgeon and was told that I looked fantastic as Justin's donor. I knew that God was guiding the process and I just had to thank Him over and over for letting things go so well and for giving me the honor of being Justin's donor. The team was scheduled to present me to the committee that Thursday and once I got the final and official approval, they would schedule the surgery date for a Monday in September. It was August and they were talking about transplant in September. I couldn't believe it.

We were thrilled and also terrified. We were excited and hopeful for that step as it would allow Justin to finally take that giant stride forward. It would allow him to get back to being a teenager. It would allow him to feel okay for more than just a few moments or hours at a time. It would allow him to have a sense of normalcy. We went through the roller coaster of emotions before with his bone marrow transplant thinking, well believing it was the answer and that Justin would be able to finally move forward. However, we were met with obstacle after obstacle and complication after complication, including kidney failure. There were many, many things that could potentially go wrong during and after surgery. I'm not a pessimist. I'm actually the opposite, but over the past few years I also became a realist. Unfortunately, my rose colored glasses were broken. They weren't just smudged or blurry, they were broken. I knew the cold, hard truth about heartache and pain. I wasn't as naïve as I had once been. I'd learned a lot about life and the reality that things didn't always work out the way I wanted them to.

I then received that phone call from Durham. The committee met and I was presented as a potential donor for Justin. The committee agreed that I met all the criteria. What a blessing and a relief that was! Justin was scheduled to be presented on the 22nd, a few days later. They were discussing late September for transplant. We were on the very edge of our seats waiting and praying. Then we got a phone call from the doctor explaining that there were some things they wanted to see improve before they went through with the transplant. We were disappointed by the news but at the same time we knew that everything was in God's hands. For one, they wanted to be sure that Justin would do okay on the anti-rejection drug, Tacrolimus. He was on Tacrolimus post-bone marrow transplant but they stopped it and put him in Cyclosporine because they wondered if the Tac was causing the neuropathy in his feet. Later, they determined that it was the chemo, Vincristine, that was responsible for the neuropathy but the doctors in Durham wanted to be sure that Justin would be okay on Tacrolimus as he would be on it for the rest of his life. In addition, they wanted to give Justin the boost of bone marrow cells so his platelets were at a better place. After his kidney transplant, Justin would be on some medications that would suppress his red and white blood cells as well as his platelets so they wanted to be sure they had him at a good place beforehand. The doctors felt that the boost of bone marrow cells should help with red blood cell and platelet production. They also wanted to be sure his lungs were clear of any pneumonia and that his BK Virus from a year ago was really gone. So it looked like transplant would be pushed back to October. We were disappointed but it was only another month.

The next day we were in Cary, North Carolina to help Ryan Brewer with a USA baseball game but Justin had a rough day and we ended up leaving the game early. He was so tired of feeling bad all the time. It broke my heart. He hardly slept as he was constantly cramping in his hands and legs. The cramps got so bad that he would lunge out of bed trying to stretch out and get some relief. He took mustard "shots" and drank dill pickle juice but that only helped for a brief time. His nephrologist couldn't figure out why he was cramping so badly. His electrolytes were in the normal range. The doctor seemed to be at a loss. He took tums as well but it didn't help - nothing did. In addition to the cramping, he had bone pain and usually needed pain meds at all hours of the night. His nausea came and went all day and night. He was tired all the time because he just couldn't rest. I thought, "One of these days, Solly - one of these days."

CHAPTER 27

A week later, at the end of August I loaded up Justin in the car at 1:00 AM and drove north to Durham. I was concerned about falling asleep while driving. Not only did I not fall asleep but I wasn't even tired. It didn't matter what time it was – if Justin started running a fever that exceeded his limit (101.5), we were off to the hospital for an automatic admittance with the standard antibiotics. And I can't think of a single time that once Justin started running a fever it didn't climb to and exceed the parameter. We arrived in Durham around 2:45 AM. Justin's oxygen levels fell and the nurses were rushing to get him on oxygen. He started complaining of severe chest pain and I knew right away that he had pneumonia. An X-ray an hour later confirmed that. He threw up several times, had body aches and a fever. They drew labs and all of his counts were low. His red blood was 7.2, they were transfusing anything under 8, his platelets were 15k and his white blood was 2.3. He was a sick kiddo. They had a hard time keeping his oxygen up. He was on a mask with a heavy flow of oxygen. In addition, his blood pressure had been low all day. They gave him a unit of platelets and then 2 units of blood. His fever broke for a few minutes but it climbed up again.

Justin was taken to ICU because his right lung was partially collapsed and he couldn't breathe. Because of his difficulty breathing, the CO_2 built up in his blood, causing more acid in his blood. They put him on the BiPAP machine in ICU, which would force air into his lungs and hold them open as he took breaths. We learned that he tested positive for gram negative rods in his blood stream, meaning he had a bacterial infection in his blood. His pneumonia was worse as well, which could have had to do with all of the fluid they had to give him from red blood cells and platelets. He was having trouble resting because of the BiPAP machine and because one of his meds caused him to itch all over. Justin was very, very sick.

This is the way it is with the business of cancer - you never know what road it, or its effects, will lead you down. The walk to ICU was sure a tough one to make, and that instance would make the 4th time we trudged down those bleak halls. Soon after you find out that your child has to be taken to ICU, a football team of doctors, nurses, respiratory therapists and the like flood into the hospital room to assess his condition. There simply wasn't enough space for everyone in Justin's room and the expanse of people spilled into the hall. I just stared at them all trying to process how in the world we ended up here again. One by one they introduced themselves, every name escaping me moments later. They all explained their intent. They were all incredibly kind but I was lost somewhere inside my own head. I met Justin's eyes, reassuring him, letting him know I was right there and going with him. I trailed the pack as they made their way to ICU, where again even more doctors flooded the room. I hung back, but still ever close, watching and giving them space to do what they needed to do to save Justin's life. They all fell into a rhythm, ducking and weaving around each other, never missing a beat. They could tell I was tense and unsure and made it a point to throw a reassuring word or gesture my way, some even attempted adding levity to the extreme situation we found ourselves in. Justin's doctor was right there, ever present. There was a moment, after everyone filed out of the room having completed their assigned tasks, when Justin, muffled through his BiPAP mask, asked me where Dr. Smith was. I explained that he was sitting right behind me on the computer. Before I knew it, Dr. Smith was standing beside me, reassuring Justin, letting him know he was there. Justin trusted him and knew if he was close, everything that could be done was being done. As things finally began to quiet down, I was left with my own thoughts. I prayed and prayed. I explained to God, not that I needed to as He knew my heart, that I was mad at Him - that Justin had been through so much and I knew He could heal him completely, so to please just do that. In the back of my mind I knew what He would have said if He was standing in front of me. He would have explained that Justin was being used for His glory and all healing would be in His time. Trust me - in my head, I knew that was true. But as a mom, it is absolutely gut wrenching to watch your child suffer and wonder how much more he could take.

I begged Justin to hang on, just awhile longer. I knew he was so tired. He was spent from fighting for so long but I pled with him to just keep fighting. I worried that at some point it would all be too damn much. He'd crossed that line of "too much" several times. I guess I just worried that he would realize it. I worried that he would tell me what he told me soon after his initial diagnosis, after just 2 weeks of chemo – that it was too hard and he couldn't do it anymore. He had been through so much since then. He had been to hell and back, but he never said it again. He never asked to quit. He may have wanted to some days but if he did I never knew about it.

I read the messages on his Facebook page to him hoping to comfort him. As I read message after message, I looked over and watched a tear slide from the corner of his eye over his BiPAP mask.

The next day the doctors were left shocked when they looked at Justin's X-ray. They thought that the pneumonia would have worsened but were "very surprised" to see the marked improvement! I, however, was not surprised. So many people stormed Heaven for Justin and I know that God heard our prayers. Justin still had a long way to go but he was improving! He was moved back to the BMT floor and soon after they identified the bacteria in his bloodstream. It was acinetobactor. It can be very resilient to antibiotics but seemed to be responding to the 3 antibiotics they had Justin on. He was getting 2 platelet transfusions a day. His right lung was improving but then they saw something in the left so he was scheduled to have a CT scan the following day to have a better look. He was on 15 hours of dialysis a day and on BiPAP only at night, unless the CT scan were to show something different.

While at the hospital, Justin's doctor came to talk to us about his kidneys. He felt that Justin's best chance, on the kidney side of things, was a study that was led by a doctor at the University of Louisville. She had done a lot of research and had a great deal of success with chimerism and tolerance in solid organ transplantation. Essentially, what they wanted to do was give Justin my marrow as well as my kidney. Giving him my marrow would, potentially, help keep his body from rejecting my kidney and could mean that he wouldn't have to be on anti-rejection drugs for the rest of his life. He would be a hybrid of Jessica, his donor, and my marrow. He would only be given enough to mine of trick his body into accepting the transplanted kidney. With all of that said, because of Justin's other conditions, he didn't qualify for the study. Justin's Durham doctor asked the doctor in Kentucky to grant Justin Compassionate Use. Compassionate Use is a way for people with life threatening illnesses to get access to experimental treatments. Justin was struggling with so many things that it was hard for anyone to know what would be best for him.

I felt like I was asleep for so long. I felt like I lived in a fog. I thought I'd seen bad things, hurtful things, and scary things. I thought I'd had a good relationship with God. I thought I knew what this life was about. I thought I had it all figured out. And then Justin got sick. The fog started to lift. I became aware of things I never knew before. I think I'm a pretty educated person, but I learned words I'd never heard before. I learned about jobs I never knew existed and specialized care. I saw pain and suffering surpass all limits of understanding. I learned that there is some pain so deep that medication cannot alleviate it. I learned that things are not black and white at all, that they are a million shades of grey. I learned that sometimes when doctors refer to 1% or 5% of patients, they are referring to your child every time. I learned what it really felt like to have your heart break. I learned what real fear is, not the stuff you see in movies but rather the things you see in ICU. I learned that God is always there, always listening, always ready for me to come to Him and that when I'm at my absolute lowest, He lifts me up. I learned that He surrounded me with exactly the right people to help Him do that, to help Him lift me up. I learned what real faith is. I learned that I know nothing of God's plans - that I have nothing figured out. That it was never about me. I learned that there is always hope and that hope is one of the strongest things you can possess.

We thought that Justin would be discharged but they decided to keep him another week. The doctors were still concerned about his infection and his pneumonia. He was feeling better for the most part but still battling pneumonia and still had to have blood and platelet transfusions daily.

Then they tested Justin for MRSA. "MRSA is a bacterium responsible for several difficult-to-treat infections in humans and is especially troublesome in hospitals where patients with open wounds, invasive devices, and weakened immune systems are at greater risk of infection than the general public."[17] Justin had 2 catheters, one in his chest and the other in his stomach. He had an open sore below the catheter in his stomach. We weren't sure what it is from but we knew that a nurse from dialysis used Chlorhexidine on him and he is allergic to that. The sore could have been from his skin breaking down because of his allergy or because they were using some strong things to clean that area and it could just be agitated. In any case, he was on isolation for the following 24 hours until they got some results back. I was concerned because his blood pressure was dropping again. It wasn't too low but it was low for him. Also, his oxygen seemed to be dropping a bit as well. The MRSA testing came back negative and Justin slowing began feeling better. A week later he was discharged from the hospital.

CHAPTER 28

It takes a while for me to process information, especially when it's difficult to swallow. We went back to Durham in early October to talk kidney transplant. Justin's primary doctor, Dr. Smith, was working diligently at trying to figure out the best course of action for him. He talked with us about two options they were looking at closely. The first we referred to as the Kentucky Way and the second as the Durham Way. Both options were looking at immune tolerance for Justin's transplanted kidney. They were hoping to optimize the life of his new kidney once he received it. Transplanted kidneys can last anywhere from 5-15 years. They would have liked to help Justin keep his kidney for longer than that by using immune tolerance, which should allow him to come off of anti-rejection drugs after a year or so, thus prolonging the life of his kidney. The ironic thing about the anti-rejection drugs is that they damage the kidneys. With the Kentucky Way, they would give Justin some of my marrow in addition to my kidney. He would keep his donor's marrow and would get just enough of mine to keep him from rejecting his new kidney. In order to do this, they would have to give him some chemo and possible radiation to knock back his current marrow enough to let my marrow come in and get settled.

With the Durham Way, they would get rid of his donor's marrow completely and replace it with mine as well as my kidney. From previous testing we knew that I was only a half match for Justin. The colleagues his doctor spoke with said they do haplo (half matched) bone marrow transplants often and with great success. Doctors at Johns Hopkins have "...developed a procedure called a half-matched bone marrow transplant that has been successful in "curing" patients of some cancers. Rather than wiping out a patient's immune system before transplanting donor bone marrow, doctors administer just enough chemotherapy to suppress the immune system, which keeps patients from rejecting the donated marrow without harming their organs."[18] Justin's case would be a bit different as he'd already had a bone marrow transplant and many complications. This choice would also require chemo, more chemo than the Kentucky Way, and possible radiation. He would get a second, complete bone marrow transplant and shortly after, a kidney transplant. I couldn't imagine how Justin could possibly endure another bone marrow transplant. I worried that the chemo and radiation would just be too much. It nearly killed him the first time around.

The doctors were leaving no stone unturned as they searched for what would work best for Justin. He was just so complicated and so unlike any other patient. It was hard to know what would work and what may kill him.

The doctors spoke to the doctor in Kentucky and she sounded interested in trying to help Justin but was looking into how to do that exactly. Apparently "Compassionate Use" was off the table but they were still collaborating with doctors from North Carolina to Kentucky to Chicago, and elsewhere in the country, to determine how to best help Justin. We were thankful for their collaboration and we knew that God was guiding the expedition whether the doctors realized it or not.

He had to have surgery at the end of October because the tube in his stomach used for dialysis had flipped again. He had two incisions in his stomach on the right side. He was leaking through them for a short time but soon stopped. However, we didn't realize that he was still leaking internally. His dialysis stopped working and he noticed a large pocket of fluid on the right side of his stomach where the incisions were, in addition to other places. He put on 14+ pounds of fluid and we immediately worried about his lungs, as he'd gone into respiratory distress from too much volume many times. They did a 3 hour hemodialysis session on him and pulled off 7 pounds of fluid and would do the same thing the following day. Then we would have to go to Durham 3 times a week for the 2 following weeks for more hemodialysis until the incisions in his stomach healed. During our lunch conversation after his release from the hospital I said, "Life sure isn't what I expected." To which he replied, "It's better, isn't it?"

It's funny how we adapt to things. A life of hospitals and medications, dialysis and tests, worry and anxiety was abnormal once. I wondered back then how we would adapt and change as it pushed and pulled to mold us into completely different people than we were before. I started to feel like that was our new normal. It seemed like a second life almost. The life we had before felt like a distant memory. As I was getting dressed one morning I noticed how many of my sweatshirt sleeves were stained with mascara. I thought of the stories those sleeves could tell about the tears and the pain they absorbed. Those stains that remained served as a reminder of where we had been and where we had still yet to go. We were forever changed.

CHAPTER 29

Thanksgiving of 2013 was the first Thanksgiving in 2 years that Justin wasn't in the hospital and we had so much to be thankful for. One of Justin's closest friends, Shane, skipped the holiday with his family and came to spend it with us in North Carolina. The love that Justin's friends had for him was so deep.

*"I can't explain in words how much Solly means to me and how much he has impacted my life simply by the way he has lived his. Through his journey I have learned and grown so much. During the highs, the lows and everything in between, I never saw the person he was change. He stayed positive and true to himself when he had every right to complain and become a totally different person. He is the strongest and most unselfish person I know and he truly gave me someone to look up to in so many ways. I thank God every day for putting such a special person in my life. I know it wasn't by accident. He has touched the hearts and souls of thousands of people to make them become better. Rather than just giving in, he took cancer and all the struggles he faced as a way to positively impact others around him in ways he will never know." –*Shane Woodson

Justin's friends sometimes talked about the impact he made on their lives. But I don't think they ever quite realized the effect they had on his. They were the difference for him and like Shane stated, I know that it was no accident that they were all friends.

On December 16th my second grandson, Jayce, was born. I was so happy that we could be there for his birth. And of course I fell in love with the little guy before he ever entered the world but seeing him made me fall a little harder. It amazed me, my capacity to love. I have three children and never imagined I could love any humans so much. Then Jordan had two beautiful grandsons and I loved them more deeply than I thought possible. I kept wondering where all of that love came from and how I possessed so much of it to give. But there we were, all in that one room at the hospital with all the people I loved most in the world – my parents, my children and my grandsons. Life was good and I was grateful. The rest of 2013 was fairly uneventful and we were completely okay with that.

CHAPTER 30

Have you ever literally waited for the other shoe to drop? When things are going well, you squint your eyes and tense up and just kind of wait. For the better part of 3 years Justin was quite literally in the hospital more than he was out of it. And when he was out, within a week or two he was being admitted again for one reason or another. So when a month went by and Justin hadn't been in the hospital, I started to get a little uneasy. How sad is that? Hesitantly, we scheduled a trip back to New Mexico for the middle of January. Some guys came together to pull off a hunt of a lifetime for Justin in Chama, New Mexico. He would be hunting buffalo. Justin was so excited he couldn't sleep. The morning we planned to drive to Chama for the hunt, Justin woke up with a fever (ah – there's that shoe!). As mentioned before, protocol for Justin was admittance if the fever reached the magical number of 101.5. It always did so we were all worried that we would have to abort the hunt. I asked for prayers right away as we drove to urgent care. While we were there, his fever started to come down. His blood pressure was pretty low but the doctor in North Carolina gave us the green light for the hunt, saying to watch him closely. Justin got to go stay at an amazing place in Chama with a couple of his closest friends and the men who made the hunt possible. It was an incredible few days.

Once back in North Carolina, we continued Justin's regular visits to Durham. I can't say enough how much I appreciate and love Justin's doctors and nurses there. We felt blessed that they took such good care of Justin and listened to our concerns. Justin began to feel like he had to move forward. He couldn't remain in limbo any longer even though we understood why we were there for so long. The best option for Justin was to go through the protocol out of Kentucky, but we had been waiting to hear back from a surgeon in Chicago, Dr. Kennedy, who was involved in that protocol, to no avail. I asked Justin's doctor if we could go to Chicago and talk to him face to face. He said he would look into it and let us know. Waiting was so hard and Justin seemed to be doing better, not being admitted so frequently to the hospital. We thought maybe it was time to make things happen.

"A life spent waiting or a life filled with stories. The choice remains yours." –Tyler Knott Gregson

Justin wanted a life filled with stories.

Mid-February Justin was admitted to the hospital in Durham. He'd been having severe diarrhea, vomiting, and extreme fatigue. He tested positive for C Diff (Clostridium Difficile – a bacterium that causes swelling and irritation in the colon) and Norovirus (an infection that causes severe vomiting and diarrhea). He was so sick. He couldn't keep anything down or in so they started him on fluids as they worried he was severely dehydrated. He had been doing so well. He needed things here and there but hadn't really been sick. Of course he always had that nausea but everything escalated so quickly and he was flat sick. The first thing we both thought of was the setback it would cause for getting a kidney. That damn shoe was dropping again. I read somewhere about a condition (Cherophobia, I believe) where people are afraid to be too happy for fear something bad might happen soon after – the proverbial shoe dropping. I never understood that before but I could absolutely understand it now. He was discharged from the hospital but wasn't better.

When he was born, he was seldom still. He was in constant motion moving from one toy to the next, one sport to the next - until he fell in love with baseball. He rarely stopped talking or smiling as he grew older. He was the happiest kid, never letting anyone or any situation get him down. He always made others laugh and feel better. Justin was, in a word, energy. But that cancer stuff was taking a toll. He had been handling it all relatively well given everything he had been through. He was still smiling. He continued to have a great attitude - but for how long? When would it all be too much? After a difficult time walking up the stairs to his room one day, Justin paused over his trash can to throw up and then slunk down onto his bed. "You know what sucks?" he asked, "...that I don't even remember what feeling good felt like." I was a broken hearted mom for my broken son.

Justin continued to struggle a great deal over the following weeks. He wasn't able to eat and was still throwing up and having diarrhea to the point that we were concerned about dehydration again. We started him on Ensure Complete for nutrition and fluids as well as yogurt to try to help fight off the bad bacteria in his gut. It was ruthless stuff and he was miserable.

Some interesting things happened around that same time. I grew even more tired of waiting for someone to contact us about Justin's kidney transplant (I'm not the most patient person) so I decided to just call the surgeon in Chicago, Dr. Kennedy. This man was a highly qualified and well-renowned surgeon and I had no idea what to expect. I just took a chance and called him. To my surprise, he actually called me back. I could see God's hand working for Justin that day. I know God worked for Justin every day but that day I could see it. Dr. Kennedy and I spoke for about 20 minutes and when all was said and done he asked me how I was able to contact him. He said he thought I was someone else when he called me back but agreed to look at Justin's records to see if he could get him into the protocol out of Kentucky. I knew that was God working and more and more I had the feeling that we were on the right path for Justin. For a while I found myself trying to guess God's intentions, trying to read His mind or rather just figure out what things meant; why I met the people I met, why Justin had the doctors and nurses he had, why his body made no sense, why things got prolonged, why I was able to reach the doctor in Chicago, why Justin had the friends he had and why I'd come to love them as my own, etc. I found myself trying to figure out His plan. It was almost comical and might be if it weren't so true. I took notice of nearly everything that happened and tried to figure out what it meant. I tried to figure out it if meant Justin would be okay or not and I noticed that I pushed against everything that leaned towards "not".

Justin and I made frequent trips to Durham because his C Diff and Norovirus just weren't improving. It got so bad that he couldn't even keep the Ensure down. We were worried and although we were still doing dialysis, we started using the lowest dextrose so we wouldn't pull off any fluid and dehydrate him even more. Doing it that way still removed the waste in his body but didn't pull off too much fluid. He couldn't shake his infections and on March 7th he was admitted. He had several procedures to try to figure out why he couldn't shake his infections and to see if there was something else going on. The doctors took biopsies, looking for GVHD (graft versus host disease). They saw a couple of polyps that they biopsied to be sure they were nothing serious. They kept him for a few days giving him fluids and doing dialysis to try to get him to a stable place and then they discharged him. We were thankful as Justin's best friend, Brady, was visiting. Justin was still miserable, even after discharge. He still couldn't eat and he couldn't take his meds. He was constantly throwing up. I was thinking they were going to have to put an NG (Nasogastric) intubation tube in for nourishment and medication purposes but that hadn't happened yet. Brady was such a good friend. He lay around and watched TV with Justin when Justin couldn't move, which was a lot of the time, and he went wherever Justin could manage when he would get a short burst of energy.

CHAPTER 31

A few days later Justin's Durham doctor called me. He went over the biopsy results which were fine, no evidence of GVHD. It was great news but that wasn't the only reason he was calling. The nephrologists, bone marrow doctors and surgeons all met about Justin the day before concerning his transplant. The surgeons decided that they didn't want to transplant Justin as he was deemed too risky. He had a myriad of complications and they honestly didn't think he would survive it. Justin's doctor, Dr. Smith, explained to them that Justin would rather attempt transplant and die than live how he had been living. That made no difference. We were told that we would more than likely need to take Justin to a different hospital. They were thinking Chicago but hospitals in California and Massachusetts were in the talks as well.

That news was monumental to Justin. He had been working hard towards transplant and he desperately wanted to move forward with his life. He felt terrible every day and he just wanted a chance at some form of normal. He would love to go one day without nausea or have the energy to walk down the street. He started off with this enormous rock of hope. It stood so strong and resilient. It stood beautiful and solid. However, as time went on and as Justin was knocked back - one step here, 2 steps there - that rock of hope was chiseled down. It was much smaller now and weaker. It wasn't gone by any means but I had to wonder how much of it Justin saw himself holding onto. It's easy to say "be strong" and man, at first we had that nailed down. We were so strong – we managed to rise above blow after blow and I was confident that we would again. I know it's natural to tell those who struggle to just keep hope alive. We did that. I spent every waking hour trying to help Justin do that - trying to remind him what he was fighting for and what he loved so much. But year after year of dealing with that can wear on someone and it was only natural for Justin to feel that way. Justin cried when I told him what his doctor said and another piece of that once so strong and stout rock of hope crumbled and fell. I frantically picked it up and tried to mash it back into place. I desperately begged Justin to not give up. I told him that we would find the right hospital and the doctors who would do the transplant. I plead with him to just hold on.

The following morning I awoke to Justin's voice screaming "MOOOOOOOOOOOM!!!!!" in my head. It jerked me out of my sleep and I ran into his room to check on him. He was okay. But I felt like it was Justin begging me to figure things out and help him. I sat down and talked with Justin the following day. I told him that we needed to consider what the doctors in Durham said concerning why they were hesitant to transplant. I wanted us to stop and think about what the doctors told us. I expressed my fear of losing him. I selfishly explained that I would rather have him living (albeit a very limited life) than risk losing him entirely. As a mother I couldn't conceive that possibility. Justin and I were sitting beside each other on the bed as we were talking. Tears began their slow descent down my cheeks, falling onto my shorts. With wisdom far beyond his years, he began explaining to me that what he was currently doing wasn't living at all. He expressed that he would rather risk everything for something than continue on the way he was living. Going to the hospital weekly and coming home to lie on the couch because he was too sick and weak to do anything wasn't any kind of life he wanted to live. Then in good Justin style he made me laugh. He said, "Haven't you ever heard the phrase - you gotta risk it for the biscuit?" With a chuckle I explained that I hadn't heard that saying. Justin said, "Sometimes you have to take big risks if you ever want the rewards." And then he asked me to research doctors and hospitals as I'd done for his bone marrow transplant to find a place who would give him a chance. And I consented. I couldn't argue with his reasoning. He was completely right and it was selfish of me to want him to exist but not really live. I knew we were looking at having to move, at least for a while. I knew that God would lead us where we needed to go and that He would provide a way while we were there. I just asked for some extra strength for the way. We were both so tired and I couldn't imagine picking up and moving again – once more leaving our family and friends behind.

The day after was another rough day. A lot of tears were shed. There was just so much we were trying to get figured out. I was on the phone with the doctor in Chicago for about an hour that morning and felt that overall, the conversation went well. Dr. Kennedy was shocked at what a complicated patient Justin was, but he seemed like he genuinely wanted to try to help. He was supposed to get back to us by that next Monday. We went to Durham for an appointment for Justin that same day and were told, once again, that the surgeons weren't comfortable with operating on Justin.

He was lying in the hospital bed getting infusions and staring off. I asked him what he was thinking about. He said, "The one thing that worries me about dying is leaving you. I don't want to leave you, Mom." That's so like Justin, to be worried about me instead of himself. All I could do was hold his hand and sob. I wanted to believe with my entire being that Justin would make it through this. He had to. I needed everyone to believe that too, for him and for me.

CHAPTER 32

We finally received some good news! Justin had been begging the doctors to remove the double lumen Vas-Cath that he had in his chest for nearly 2 years. They finally agreed and they called with a surgery time for the following week. He only needed that Vas-Cath for emergency hemodialysis, which he hadn't needed in a while. The doctors would have to put a port back in but at least he would be able to shower and swim! We didn't live far from the beach and he so missed swimming! When we went to the beach he could only sit on the beach and put his feet in the water. He also missed showering. He'd been taking baths for so long that he'd gotten used to it but he definitely wished he could shower.

Justin was lying in bed that night feeling so miserable after throwing up for the umpteenth time. He just couldn't find any relief. I had given him all the meds I could, he had a cold washrag on his head and eyes, he tried some Sprite and I was rubbing his back. He was rocking back and forth trying to find some comfort and I felt so completely helpless. I was racking my brain trying to think of some other thing I could do for him and then I felt so stupid for forgetting the most important thing. I reached out and held his hand and we just prayed and prayed for some relief - for a peaceful night's rest for Justin and for healing from the symptoms of that Norovirus. We pled with God to touch Justin and take the Norovirus and its symptoms from him. Then Justin drifted off to sleep as I continued to watch some TV. Justin slept through the entire night, never waking up to throw up! The next morning he woke up with an appetite. We were thanking the Lord for answered prayers. Justin had lost so much weight in a few weeks because of that illness. It was wrecking him. The reprieve didn't last long as he had another rough day not soon after. His throwing up became violent and left his muscles and throat seriously hurting.

That night he had a decent rest but within an hour of being awake, he threw up three times. That Norovirus was nasty but we continued to pray for healing from the symptoms. He was scheduled for surgery on the following Thursday to have his Vas-Cath removed and a port placed.

While at the hospital they did a test on Justin that measured his PRA (Panel Reactive Antibody). "PRA is an immunological laboratory test routinely performed on the blood of people awaiting organ transplantation. The PRA score is expressed as a percentage between 0% and 99%. It represents the proportion of the population to which the person being tested will react via pre-existing antibodies. These antibodies target the Human Leukocyte Antigen (HLA), a protein found on most cells of the body."[19]

According to WebMD, "A high PRA usually means that the person is primed to react immunologically against a large proportion of the population. Individuals with a high PRA are often termed "sensitized", which indicates that they have been exposed to "foreign" (or non-self) proteins in the past and have developed antibodies to them. These antibodies develop following previous transplants, blood transfusions and pregnancy. Transplanting organs into recipients who are "sensitized" to the organs significantly increases the risk of rejection, resulting in higher immunosuppressant requirement and shorter transplant survival. People with high PRA therefore spend longer waiting for an organ to which they have no pre-existing antibodies."[20] Thus, a high PRA percentage for Justin would set us back greatly.

It was an important test when awaiting transplant. At one point when they tested him it was 60%, and then when they tested him the week after – it was negative. We felt like we were on the right path with transplant and that God's hand was on Justin. The doctor in Chicago, Dr. Kennedy, called the following day. After reviewing Justin's medical files and talking to the transplant team, they wanted us to go to Chicago to meet with them. We would go sometime in the following 2 months when, God willing, Justin got some relief from that Norovirus.

After Justin's surgery, the surgeon came out to tell me that the vein he wanted to go through in Justin's neck, for his port, wasn't there. He said that when someone has lines and ports and such, veins can disappear. He ended up putting Justin's port right below his right nipple. Justin woke up in a tremendous amount of pain due to the 3 incisions that were made: one to remove the Vas-Cath, one to search for that vein and one for his port. On top of that, the anesthesiologist once again used a drug on Justin that he is allergic to. We went over this drug a minimum of 10 times collectively with every single person that was going to be in the operating room with Justin. Needless to say, I was frustrated.

That evening Justin still couldn't eat, he was throwing up regularly and his weight loss was at 17 pounds. We were in agreement that he needed to be admitted for TPN, to give him nutrients that he wasn't getting. He was scheduled to go in Monday after his clinic visit to be admitted for a few days to try to get him some nutrition. I was relieved that Justin was going to get some help. I knew that he had to be malnourished because he just couldn't keep anything down and he'd been so sick for over a month.

The night before he was scheduled to go in and be admitted, things went sideways with Justin and I worried that maybe it had gone on too long.

CHAPTER 33

I discovered a different kind of terror. It's funny how you think you have felt the height of an emotion, or all the angles of that emotion and then something happens and you feel things that you have never felt before. Of course, I'd felt terror and I saw things with Justin the past nearly 3 years that broke me but when I heard that thud and I walked in to see my son having a seizure, I felt a different side of terror. He had been lying in bed with me. He was rocking which was normal for him. He laid in the fetal position and rocked to try to ease his symptoms. I was watching TV and Tripp had come in the room and crawled onto the bed beside Justin. He tried to move Justin's arm from over his face and asked, "What's wrong with Juju?" Tripp knew something wasn't right. Soon after, I helped Justin to the bathroom, as he was always too weak to walk on his own. I closed the door and waited in the hall telling him to let me know when he was ready - I was right outside in the hall. Minutes later I heard a thud, solid and loud. I said Justin's name loudly but there was no response. I threw open the door and Justin was lying on his side, convulsing. He had fallen off the toilet and hit his head on the wall. His pajama bottoms and underwear were around his ankles. He was unresponsive and rigid. His jaw was clenched tight. I yelled downstairs for my parents to call 911 and get an ambulance there. My dad came rushing into the hall just outside the bathroom asking what he could do. I was on my knees holding Justin the best way I could. I was crying and scared. And then I just started to pray. Prayer – once again it's all I had and all I could do. My faith had been tested for 3 years, I won't deny that. There is so much I don't understand, although I know that I won't understand this side of heaven. But when all the chips were down and I was grasping for something, I gripped onto my faith and to God. I begged Him to let Justin be okay. Justin finally came to but had no recollection of what had happened. Within seconds the fire department arrived and came upstairs to assess Justin. He was screaming about pain in his back. He looked so scared. My daughter showed up soon after and the ambulance minutes after that. They got Justin out of the bathroom and put him on a chair of sorts to get him downstairs. They then put him on a stretcher and loaded him into the ambulance; all the while he was still having back pain. I clambered into the ambulance with him with a frozen look of confusion mixed with fear on my face. They gave Justin something immediately to help him with his anxiety and with the pain as well. Jenna said she would meet me at the hospital and we were off. I looked around the ambulance we were in, I looked at the back of my son's head and listened as he rattled off the many medications he was on and I felt hot tears slide down my cheeks – tears I wasn't even aware I was crying. We arrived at the emergency room in Charlotte and his primary doctor was notified immediately. They monitored him closely until the ambulance from Durham arrived several hours later to take him to his primary hospital – the only place we really felt at ease with him.

There we were, back at the hospital and Justin was having every test under the sun performed on him. He wasn't sleeping much because of the tests and the constant stream of doctors coming in and out of his room. His back pain was being managed but his nausea and vomiting were still at an all-time high. They started him on TPN so I was hoping that would help. Justin's lungs became an issue as the doctors could hear some fluid and worried he may have had pneumonia or a collapsed lung again.

A couple of days later had Justin feeling much better. His tests came back okay and the doctors thought it was a combination of dehydration, malnutrition and blood pressure issues that contributed to his seizure. The MRI on his back showed several compression fractures. They could have been from a few months previous but they think that his back pain came from swelling around those fractures pushing on the nerves from when he fell during his seizure.

After being discharged, Justin had to go see the eye doctor as they discovered that he had a bad hemorrhage in his right eye. They thought that when he had his seizure and hit his head it caused a hemorrhage in his eye. They said that his eyes would bleed easily because of the abnormal vessels. He got a shot in his eye to temporarily dry up the bleed but they scheduled him for laser surgery a month later to cauterize the blood vessels and try to prevent further bleeds.

CHAPTER 34

I spoke with Dr. Kennedy in Chicago again on the phone. He asked me what led us to him and I explained what Justin had gone through and that I felt like he was who could help Justin – that I needed *someone* to help him. He scheduled us for an appointment in Chicago for June 17th. They wanted us to attend a workshop that morning on kidney transplant and then one on living donor transplant. After both of those meetings, we would have appointments with the transplant surgeon and a nephrologist to evaluate Justin. While it was substantial news and we are eternally grateful that they wanted to see Justin and were contemplating transplanting him, we still needed to be sure that it was the right path - that it was the path that God wanted us on.

The first thing we had to do was find a way to be able to afford to travel to and live wherever it was we were headed (our focus being on Chicago). Jenna organized a 5K run in Boone, NC in the middle of May and we had a tremendously wonderful turnout. Justin walked nearly the entire 5K, pushing his wheelchair across the finish line, rather than riding in it. Likewise, a couple of amazing friends put on the exact same run but in Farmington, NM. We sold T-shirts and had raffles. The communities in Boone and Farmington came together once again to help my son get the care he needed. It was so touching and I was again moved by humanity.

We had been going hard and fast since July of 2011, when Justin was first diagnosed with cancer - hospital after hospital, admittance after admittance and complication after complication. As I mentioned, we waited with bated breath for the proverbial "other shoe to drop." We soaked up those moments in between and lived in them as best we could but we knew it wouldn't be long before something else happened, because it was inevitable - something always happened. It wasn't so much that we were being pessimists as much as we were just being realists. But days came and went and rather than being admitted, Justin just continued to feel a little bit better.

It had been a month and a half since Justin's seizure, the last of that nasty Norovirus and his last admittance and he actually felt good. He had energy and felt like doing things, rather than just moving from his bed to the couch. At first, I was constantly asking him if he needed a trash can to throw up in as he had spent so much time doing just that. It was just a knee jerk reaction every time he moved. That passed and I saw light in his eyes and a smile that became more prevalent daily. That's not to say that he didn't struggle with some side effects still. He did, but the change in him was evident. I had to think, I had to wonder if it was just affirmation that we were heading in the right direction with Chicago and that God was building his strength to prepare him for the next stage.

The normal days were such a gift. It was unusual to have him sleeping in his own room and not worry about him throwing up or respiratory failure or fevers or pain. It was odd to be able to sleep and really rest. How sad it was that those things were unusual or odd. I found myself wondering if and when something would come crashing down. Of course, I basked in those days when he was feeling well but after 3 years of obstacle after obstacle, it was natural to worry and wonder. I believed though, that Justin was being prepared for his next fight and that he would need all the strength and good days that he could muster to bring him through what lay ahead.

We found ourselves doing normal-ish things like running errands and spending more time with our family. We had more time to go and do since Justin wasn't being admitted every other week. When Justin was healthy I told him many times how there was no where I'd rather have been than watching him play baseball. I caught him staring at me as we were driving down the road and I asked him what he was thinking. He said, "I was thinking how I miss you watching me play baseball." My heart ached to watch him play again. I know it tore him up to have that taken from him. I know that he struggled every day with it but especially during baseball season. We still went to games but it was bittersweet for both Justin and me. On the one hand, we both flat loved baseball. Sure, he loved it more than me, but not by much. We loved it for different reasons, I guess. I remember when he was in middle school, one of his teachers asked the kids what they wanted to do when they were older and Justin said "play baseball." It's all he ever said because it's all he ever wanted to do. I'd spent years telling Justin that he could do or be anything he wanted if he worked hard enough for it, which I completely believe. I always saw him playing college ball. We can read all the quotes we want about what cancer can and can't take but it did take that from Justin. Yes, I know he might still play "someday," but I also know that he missed out on going away to college with his buddies and playing baseball. That was devastating for him. I know that nothing seemed to go according to what we planned and that's because God has bigger plans for us. What he will do and where he will end up will be far better than where we envisioned him going and what we thought he would be doing. It doesn't quite take away that sting though when you are sitting in those stands watching the game that once gave reason to your being, that explained your every thought and was a constant in a world of chaos.

CHAPTER 35

On June 14th, 2014, with butterflies in our stomachs, we traveled to Chicago for meetings and Justin's evaluation. As our luck seemed to go, we were both sick. Justin's chest sounded bad and of course I worried about pneumonia. I emailed his doctor in Durham who suggested a few things but also said that if it got too bad, Justin would need to go to the emergency room. We did the tourist thing in Chicago, walking around a lot in the hopes it would help work that fluid out. We were both solemnly nervous. Justin had been turned down for transplant and we traveled 1,400 miles on literally hope and a prayer.

The following day we were at the Chicago hospital all day long. We had been to a lot of big cities by the time we found our way to Chicago. The Chicago hospital was near the water in a beautiful area. It wasn't as menacing as the hospital in Houston but it was larger than the one in Durham. We found the building we were looking for and made our way to the 19th floor. We attended one big group meeting with other potential donors and recipients where a nephrologist spoke to us about what to expect. After that we had another group meeting with a nurse practitioner. All potential recipients were then taken from the room for further testing while the donors met with a transplant surgeon, Dr. Kennedy, who happened to be the doctor I'd been speaking to for months. He also gave us information on what to expect generally speaking.

Justin and I then met with Dr. Kennedy. He remembered our in-depth conversations as well as Justin's extensive file. He examined Justin and then talked to us. He was torn. Justin was such a complicated patient. After going through everything in detail, he told us that the committee would meet to discuss Justin the following week and make a decision. He said that if they did the transplant, we would have to stay in Chicago for 3 months or more and that they could do it as soon as September. We would have to fly to Chicago at least one more time to meet with the team before we drove out if they agreed to transplant. I asked Justin what his thoughts were as we were walking back to our hotel. He said, "Well, I'm worried. I guess I didn't realize how truly risky this will be but that doctor explained it well and was very detailed." I wasn't sure what feelings of my own to interject. I didn't know what the "good" or "right" answer was – I wasn't sure there was one. We walked back to our hotel in silence, weighing our own thoughts.

Living in Chicago for 3 months or more was going to be a challenge. It was a very expensive city and Justin was no longer a child so we couldn't stay at the Ronald McDonald House. I looked into hotels, apartments and church assisted living. I'll be honest - I was worried. We had some money from several fundraisers but it wouldn't be enough. Then I received a phone call from someone who wanted to help, who said she'd been called by God to help. It was like I could hear God saying, "See, I told you I would make a way." I had chills. I was speechless. It not only put my mind at rest about the financial part of it but it also told me that Justin was *supposed* to go to Chicago and he *was* indeed supposed to have a kidney transplant. I didn't have to fight to make things happen. I didn't have to try to fit that square peg in a round hole. It all just fell together and I felt such peace.

Dr. Kennedy from Chicago called me the following week after their meeting about Justin. He said the committee talked quite extensively about his case and wanted to look at a couple of genetic tests on me to be sure that Justin didn't get his aHUS from me since I'd be giving him my kidney. If those tests came back okay, which they believed they would, they would give the green light for his transplant. It seemed as though everything was falling together almost effortlessly. I wasn't clawing and scratching to make it work. It was just working. By the grace of God, it was working.

When Justin was diagnosed with cancer, my world came crashing down around me. I didn't know how to process anything and I was in a constant state of asking, "How and why?" I was angry at God. I spoke to Him often about that. And when I went to Him, terrified in prayer, he calmed my heart and gave me peace. I remember in the beginning when people would talk to us or pray with us about Justin, they often said "Thy will be done." I remember that striking me so hard in the chest and thinking, "No, because what if *His* will is to take Justin home? What if His will takes him from me, from his dad and his brother and sister? It can't be His will, it had to be *my* will. I had to fight for Justin and fight hard because he's my son, he's my little boy and I want him here. I want to see him grow old and have children and play baseball again. I want to see him healthy and happy again. I want to always be able to hug his neck and kiss his cheek. I want to always be able to hold him."

I can't alter God's plans with those thoughts and feelings but let me say something - facing the idea of losing a child is unbearable. No parent should have to know that pain for any reason. That kind of pain is what nightmares are made of. We were at the 3 year mark and people continued to say, "Thy will be done" and I continued to cringe as they said it. I'd never been able to say it because I felt like in saying that, I was saying it was okay for God to take Justin if He needed him - not that God needed my permission.

What was funny in all of it was that God's will was being done, no matter if I gave my consent or not. Everything that happened *was* God's will and He took care of Justin. He protected him and performed miracle after miracle through him. He showed His hand on Justin and he showed us who He is. It's funny to think I had some sort of control over what was happening, and finally after 3 years, I could finally say: My God, *Thy* will be done.

CHAPTER 36

When a child gets a life-threatening illness, they are granted a wish through the Make a Wish Foundation. It can be anything from trips, to meeting someone famous, to toys and so forth. Justin was told back in 2011 that he would get a wish but he was never healthy enough to have it until that summer of 2014. We were told that we needed to take it before Justin's transplant surgery. Justin's doctors all over the country encouraged us to take it that summer because none of them were quite sure that Justin would have another opportunity. Everyone was worried about the kidney transplant. That was unsettling but I understood that it was realistic. Justin wanted to go to Hawaii for his Make a Wish. He said he wanted to do something that involved his family and he'd always wanted to snorkel and swim with dolphins. Justin craved simplicity. He decided on Hawaii and did all he wanted to do and then some. It was a good week but also bitter. It was hard to not remember why we were there and heaviness of what lay ahead. But it also made us appreciate every single moment we had, not just on that trip but all that summer. I found myself slowing down. I wasn't rushing to get on from one moment to the next. If anything, it was quite the opposite. I was trying to slow time. I was trying to live a lifetime in each moment that unfolded.

The mind and heart are funny things. It's crazy how you put your entire being into something for so long, you jump over and around hoops, and sometimes through, you move and you plan and you email and you plead with doctors and then when it becomes a reality, you go into panic mode. The day we flew home from Hawaii, I received a phone call from Dr. Kennedy in Chicago. He said he'd received my genetic testing and it all looked fine. He went on to say that I just needed to have a few more tests but that he would like to plan on doing the kidney transplant for Justin, with me as his donor, mid-August. Excitement and terror at the same time

158

make odd bed fellows, so to speak. Tears mixed with butterflies and elation mixed with terror all wrapped around me and I let out a breath I felt like I'd been holding for a very long time.

I remember the anticipation of going to Houston for Justin's bone marrow transplant. It was an odd thing to get excited about something like that but then again, I knew it was what would save his life. It seemed like such a given. Of course, we went - of course we had to, right? Justin had a rare form of Leukemia and would need a bone marrow transplant to beat it. We were so naïve as we made that drive. We were about to make another journey, this time to Chicago. That naivety had been replaced with worldliness. I knew far too much of what could happen. Every scenario played itself out in my head like a movie that just never ended right - never made sense. The ebb and flow of those scenarios increased as Justin's surgery date approached.

I was scheduled to meet with the nephrologist, Dr. Starnes, and the social worker at the hospital in Chicago on August 14th. I flew out for a quick trip on August 13th to meet with her and wrap up any loose ends in preparation for the kidney transplant. Justin and I were to have our pre-op appointments on August 21st. The surgery date was August 29th. Justin felt the best he'd felt since before his bone marrow transplant. He was strong and ready for this and I was convinced that it would be *the* difference. Justin's kidney transplant would be his turning point. On Justin's 20th birthday, August 19th, we packed the car, climbed inside and began our journey to Chicago. We were ready.

Remember that feeling of getting ready to graduate high school and knowing that you could do or be anything you wanted to be? Remember the excitement of new beginnings and exploring the unknown? I was seeing back-to-school pictures and my teacher friends preparing their classrooms for another memorable year of teaching. I remembered the life I had 3 years previous, when I thought I had some idea of what normal meant, when things made sense and the future seemed clear. It felt like another lifetime and maybe even another person living that life 3 years ago. I guess in a sense, it was. God knows I'd changed since Justin was diagnosed with cancer. I had to adapt and make it through some grueling, daunting periods along the way. We were almost on the other side of it all and I was feeling those same things I felt upon graduating from high school - like the world was ours for the taking, like we could be and do whatever we wanted, go and explore this great, big world and be whoever we wanted to be.

We made it to Chicago without incident, stopping along the way to see our family in Ohio. It was so comforting to see them. We were definitely in need of hugs and laughter. They even had a cake for Justin's birthday. After a great evening catching up, they hugged us and sent us on our way the following morning. Once arriving in Chicago, we stayed in a hotel for a week until the apartment we rented for 3 months was available. It was the hotel we always stayed in when we went to Chicago - perfect walking distance to the hospital. We had our appointments and enjoyed the city as best we could with butterflies swirling around in our stomachs and faraway thoughts dominating our minds. The apartment was a short drive from the hospital but it was in a great area. It was probably exactly what someone would picture an apartment in a big city to be like. It was on the 45th floor and was perfect for what we needed. There was one king size bed, a bathroom, a kitchen and a very small living room with a couch that folded out into a bed. It would be home for the next 3 months. We got settled in and then it was time. It felt like everywhere we went we were discovering different versions of ourselves, parts that we'd never seen before. Seeing us living in Chicago isn't something I would have ever imagined for us, but then again most things weren't that we'd been experiencing lately. We were doing it though. We rose to any occasion, staring it in the face and did the best we could. The years of cancer, chemo and complications led to what would unfold the following day.

CHAPTER 37

As Justin and I were prepped for transplant, I heard the warnings from Justin's doctors echo in my head. I worried that maybe God's will was going to be that Justin not make it through surgery. Your mind does those things – it picks the worst time to start calculating the likelihood of every possible scenario. Justin and I were both back in pre-op at the same time. Jenna was with me and Jason was with Justin. The plan was to take me back first, remove my left kidney during a 3 hour procedure and then get Justin back immediately to give him my kidney. They would not take out either of his kidneys. Rather, they would make an incision on the right side of his stomach and place the transplanted kidney up front and re-route the plumbing. Justin came over to my little stall in pre-op to hug me and tell me good luck. He sat down on my bed beside me and put his arm around me. I knew how much receiving my kidney meant to him. I understood it because I saw his need for it every day. He didn't have to thank me. He didn't have to say a word. I was his mom. It was a given and an absolute honor for me. We held hands and I told him how much I loved him and that I would see him on the other side of surgery. And then I watched him walk away. Once they took me back I wondered if I'd ever see him again. I had to push all of that aside and just believe that this was the game changer.

I woke up groggy and immediately asked about Justin. Jenna said that he was doing fine and that things went well. I was immediately at peace. Soon after, we were both taken to our hospital rooms for the night. Jenna never left me. I was in and out of sleep and on a lot of pain meds. I was told that I would be in a great deal of pain for up to 6 weeks. I didn't really believe I would hurt that badly for 6 weeks. When I felt up to it, Jenna and I walked over to Justin's room to see how he was doing. He was all smiles. I hugged him for a long while and cried. My heart enveloped that hospital room with so much love. It was a neat feeling to know that he had a piece of me inside him, helping him live normally. After 3 years, I didn't feel *quite* so helpless. Justin had a Foley catheter in and was peeing like a champ. His nurses commented that they had never seen a transplanted kidney pee so quickly and so much.

Justin and I were discharged within a couple of days and we happily went to the apartment to rest. It was quite the whirlwind. We knew that he wasn't out of the woods yet. We had to watch him closely for rejection and try to keep him healthy as his immune system would be suppressed all the time. We were both in quite a bit of pain. I found it difficult to do anything and began to wonder if it would really be a solid 6 weeks of recovery on my end. I couldn't move without cringing. It hurt to even pee as that uses abdominal muscles. At night I used a pillow pulled tight against my stomach to try to sleep. During the day, I walked hunched over, favoring my left side. After a few days, Justin was doing well and felt mostly great which left him feeling guilty that I was hurting so much. I was swollen in my stomach and legs whereas Justin had finally lost most of his swelling. Jenna and I had a concern that I may have had a blood clot in my leg so she took me to the emergency room one night. The wait was ridiculous so we went back to the apartment and hoped and prayed for the best. For 3 years I prayed and I wished that I could somehow take on what Justin was going through and even though I was *nowhere* close, it felt good to be the one hurting so Justin could feel better. That's not the martyr in me, it's the momma.

We followed the doctor's orders and walked every day to help us both heal. On the first day we started, I was hobbling along favoring my left side as I was still in a great deal of pain. Justin was walking briskly in front of me and I just stopped, stared at that walking miracle and sobbed. He stopped and turned around to wait for *me* that day. At first he thought I was crying because I was in pain but it was actually quite the opposite. I felt nothing but joy watching him. He hadn't been able to walk without support for years and there he was strolling up the streets of Chicago. On some days we would go to a park, walking a little and then sitting on the park bench absorbing the sun. Other days I only had enough energy to walk up the street from our apartment. Justin, however, had more energy than he'd had in years. It was a miracle. It was all so much more than I could have hoped for.

The difference in Justin pre and post-transplant was extraordinary. Before his transplant, he was retaining a lot of fluid and puffy everywhere. He had no energy and fought fatigue all day long. We had to stop often to let him rest when we were out walking around and he always had to lean on me to walk anywhere. He was constantly nauseated. His blood pressure was a mess to deal with and he always dreaded hooking up to his dialysis machine because it was painful and constraining. When he first got his new kidney, he started peeing through the catheter right away. He quickly lost all of the extra fluid he was holding onto and his energy steadily increased. He had some nausea but none like before. The first time he peed after having the catheter removed, he cried. He hadn't been able to pee in a year and a half. He talked of peeing with an expression of elation on his face. That night he didn't get any sleep because he was up peeing every 20 minutes. He didn't complain. He said, "I've waited for 3 years to feel like this - thank you, Mom!!" I can't tell you what it did to my heart to see him doing so well and so incredibly happy. He had some side effects from drugs that were used in the hospital as well as an allergic reaction to one they prescribed him after getting out. But even given all of that, he was doing great. The doctors said that his kidney was working fabulously. They were trying to titrate his meds to get him to a safe and comfortable place. We were so thankful to God.

We went into the hospital weekly so the doctors could monitor his labs closely. I came to quickly love and appreciate Justin's new nephrologist, Dr. Starnes, in Chicago. He was wonderful and similar to his doctors in North Carolina and Texas as he always answered my texts or emails. One of the big concerns that accompany a transplant is immunosuppression. Justin's body would be immunosuppressed, to a degree, for the rest of his life. Because of that, it's much easier for him to get sick; whether he catches something from someone else or illnesses that lie dormant become active. He became ill a couple of weeks after his kidney transplant. He had some issues with his gut and didn't have much energy so they ran some tests. He tested positive for Norovirus. That was the illness he'd had for 2 months the spring of that same year. Naturally, it worried me given all of the issues he'd had previously. I couldn't imagine a setback; I wouldn't even consider it. Thankfully, he never felt as bad as he had before.

Justin had an appointment at the end of September with Dr. Starnes. He was quite impressed with how well Justin was doing. One of his major concerns was that Justin's aHUS would flare up right after transplant. That hadn't happened so they were pleased. He had a trace of BK Virus in his urine and they continued to monitor that. His kidney was still working beautifully. His creatinine was staying around 1.1, which was perfect. They were still playing with his medications, mostly with his Prograf - that immunosuppressive drug that is used mainly after organ transplants to reduce the activity of the patient's immune system and lower the risk of organ rejection. They kept changing the dosage so it was up and down every other week. He had his staples removed and we discussed the possibility of us leaving after he got his PD catheter and stent removed in mid - October if Justin continued to do well. Of course, Justin would have to live near a transplant hospital for quite some time. He would have to be monitored closely. Going into that transplant, we made up our minds and hearts that it was going to be the difference for him. We believed that things would go right, that we would be left in shock. That's exactly what happened. We were so grateful that someone took a chance on him and gave Justin the opportunity at a normal life. We were thankful to God for preparing the way. And I was thankful to Justin for his faith.

We spent most days doing something outside. We had our walks but we also visited museums and parks. We tried to stay busy as best we could. I was often in quite a bit of pain from the surgery so we had plenty of rest time as well. Justin had an appointment with his nephrologist on October 1st to discuss going home. He had been doing so well that we went in to discuss leaving the following week. Justin's labs showed a rise in his creatinine, which had the doctors a little concerned. He had Norovirus, and with it diarrhea, so it was a possibility that he was somewhat dehydrated and that could have caused a rise in his creatinine. We were hoping that with plenty of water, he would be back to good in no time and we could stay on track for leaving.

Not long after, Justin had surgery to remove his PD catheter and I sat beside his bed just looking at him. My eyes started scanning the room, taking in everything. I wondered how many times in the past 3+ years that I sat beside his bed as he has slept, as he has screamed in pain, as he stared off into nothing. How many times did I sit with him through laughter and tears, when things seemed hopeless and when hope was all we had? How often was he hooked up to tubes, various breathing apparatuses, IVs, PCAs, multiple catheters, plasmapheresis machines, dialysis machines, leads, NG tubes, TPN and so forth? Being there that day for that purpose almost seemed dreamlike. The days of treatment had stretched into months and they stretched into years and then we found ourselves in that hospital in Chicago doing something positive that would change Justin's life for the better. The road that Justin had been on was long and grueling but we left Chicago with hope for a future for Justin.

CHAPTER 38

After years of caring for Justin 24/7, he was finally doing well and it was time for both of us to consider life after illness. Justin still had regular doctor appointments, he was still receiving Solaris infusions, he was still on a list of medications and he still had issues with side effects of chemo but comparatively speaking, he was a brand new man. All of those wishes I had for him – to walk without the need of support, to rest undisturbed from pain and to not be nauseated constantly had become realities for him. I couldn't believe that after 3 ½ years, Justin was finally nausea free for the most part. Years previous, I'd told him that someday he wouldn't be plagued with stomach issues and there was a time when I wondered if it would ever be true. It took much longer than anticipated but that day finally came. Sometimes life surprises you. Sometimes it eases up and allows those you love to recover from their illnesses and be happy and sometimes it reminds you of your strength and purpose and love.

Justin started to plan a move to Utah to live as a 20 year old with 3 of his friends. I started a job and life seemed to be heading in a different direction for us. Naturally, we should have been ecstatic and completely ready but it wasn't that easy. When Justin got sick our lives changed unexpectedly and drastically and we were utterly unprepared. But after the first year or two we acclimated to our new "normal." And as he improved every day, our lives started to shift again. For some reason I felt unprepared for that swing back towards normal. It had been months since Justin was admitted to any hospital and I decided it was time to unpack our emergency bags. I had 2 bags that remained fresh, packed and ready to go. In one I had Justin and my clothes - everything we could possibly need if he was suddenly admitted. In the second bag I had toiletry items needed for hospital stays. Upon return home from an admittance, I washed the clothes and restocked the toiletries so they would be ready to go. One day, I sat in the middle of my bedroom floor and unpacked both bags and found myself in the middle of a panic attack. I was lying in the middle of the floor sobbing and trying to catch my breath. I didn't understand it. It was a happy time. There was so much good news, but I didn't know how to live a life after what we had experienced. I didn't know how to go from fighting for my son's life to doing anything else. No other job seemed as important as taking care of my child. I used to be a teacher but who was I after all of that? Where did I fit in? On the other side of it, would Justin be okay so far away from me? What if he needed me? So many questions and uncertainties spun around in my head. I felt off balance and I was scared.

On December 5, 2014 Justin and I went back to Chicago for a kidney biopsy to be sure he wasn't rejecting his kidney and to see if that aHUS was still in check. Everything was as good as we could hope for it to be. Things were progressing smoothly and Justin was on track to move to Utah in February of 2015.

Justin's eyes continued to be an issue and he went into the doctor regularly to have the vessels cauterized. He continued to have labs and infusions every two weeks and in January he had his 4 year post-bone marrow transplant testing completed in Durham. To add to that we found out that the chemo, radiation and past pneumonias did quite a number on Justin's lungs and they weren't functioning as well as they'd hoped. They prescribed him 2 inhalers, one scheduled and one a rescue inhaler. His adrenal glands, which produce adrenaline and a variety of steroids, weren't working very well either so they put him on extra hydrocortisone. "The adrenal glands produce hormones that help the body control blood sugar, burn protein and fat, react to stressors like a major illness or injury, and regulate blood pressure."[21] They gave him hydrocortisone to take in injection form in case his body was to ever go into shock. Things weren't perfect but Justin was seeing good days and overall things were outstanding. With the help from Justin's doctors in Durham and Chicago, we were able to get his care set up at transplant hospital in Salt Lake City, about an hour from where he would be living.

In February, we packed Justin's car until it was nearly busting with everything he could possibly take and we set out on our trek from North Carolina to Utah. Again, I packed the car so Justin could recline his chair back and rest. It was going to be a long drive. I would be driving most of it as Justin's vision still wasn't the best. The plan was to take him to Utah, get him settled in and then I would fly out of Salt Lake City to Colorado to begin a job I took in the off-road industry. He gave his hugs and we said our goodbyes to our family. That too was odd. They took us in and let us stay with them while in North Carolina. Being away from them would take some getting used to.

The drive was good for us and I was thankful for that time with Justin.

Soon after, I would be leaving him, unsure when I'd see him again and that was hard to take in. The most comforting thing I had was knowing he would be living with Brady and James. I knew they would let me know immediately if something went wrong. As we drove down endless interstates we sang at the top of our lungs, we laughed and we talked about the journey Justin had been on and where life was taking him. It was good for us both. The road whizzed by as we drove farther and farther away from the life we had become accustomed to. By Wyoming, on the third day, Justin was struggling. He spiked a fever and felt generally crappy. I thought it was the drive and being in the car for so long. We decided to pull over early and get a hotel. Justin's fever steadily rose and he still had that port in his chest so we had to visit the closest hospital. It was in a small town and they weren't sure what to do so they discharged him and we just prayed his fever would break. And it did. The following day was our last day on the road and I delivered Justin to his new home. We were both exhausted.

We spent a day or two checking out his new hometown and enjoying the sights. He and Brady dropped me off at the hotel in Salt Lake City a couple of days later so I could catch my flight early that following morning. Leaving Justin was hard. It tugged exceedingly hard on my heartstrings but I knew it was what was best for him. He had been in Provo for a week but it felt like a month! I tried to not be that parent that called 27 times a day but I had to talk him at least once every day. He began doing normal things. He went grocery shopping and refilled his meds. He played poker with Brady and his family and babysat. He talked to the hospital and to insurance to get labs and his infusion set up at a hospital a little closer to him although he would still go to Salt Lake City once every 2 months. He even signed up at a gym and was working out. In a nutshell he was living life on his terms and I couldn't have been more proud! Overall, he had been feeling decent. I was definitely struggling a lot more than he was. I decided I needed to plan a visit to see him. I had to wean myself off slowly, I guess. And then something amazing happened.

The scout who drafted Justin to the Rockies, Chris Forbes, was always checking on him and would often let the team know how he was. In November of the previous year, one of the pitchers for the Rockies, Tyler Matzek contacted me about getting Justin out to Spring Training that year. He and his wife, Lauren, had been following Justin's journey and wanted to make it happen for him - an all-expense paid trip to Arizona for Spring Training. I had a hard time believing that it was going to happen but it did! We were booked to go to Arizona on March 18th, 2015 for 5 days but I had no idea what would ensue once we got there. Justin was even allowed to bring his best friend, Brady. It was a dream come true for Justin and we were deeply thankful to Tyler, Lauren, Chris Forbes and the entire Rockies organization for making it become a reality.

167

Brady and Justin flew out of Salt Lake City and I met them in Phoenix. We got checked into the hotel and then headed out to the field the following day to take in some baseball. Life is funny. I said that 100 times for 4 years. I can't express how blessed we were to have met such remarkable people. Tyler and Lauren were so wonderful to want to fly us out so Justin could be there for the Rockies Spring Training. That was a gift that touched our hearts, but they took it so far beyond that and spent time with us outside of the ball field. We had the opportunity to get to know them, to sit and talk and laugh with them and learn what absolutely incredible people they are. We saw not only incredibly talented ball players but also outstanding individuals with beautiful hearts and kind souls

Life took us back to our respective places in the country and I continued to miss Justin but I kept busy and that definitely helped. Justin continued to feel well and it continued to amaze me. One day in June of 2015, Brady sent me a picture of Justin surfing waves at the lake. I literally had to zoom in on the picture to be sure it was Justin and to see if it was a current picture of him. It was. I started crying mostly from pure amazement and partly from being terrified. I just could not find the right place in my brain that could believe he was able to do that after so much crippling pain and illness the previous 4 years. I remembered when Justin was so sick he could hardly get off the couch or out of bed. And then I realized that it wasn't in my head that I looked for that place of belief - it was in my heart. I recalled when the Durham hospital told us they wouldn't do the transplant and the absolute heart break we felt. But I also remembered sitting down and talking with Justin and how he told me he wanted me to find someone to do the transplant - that he had faith it would work out and that even if it didn't, he had to try. And then I was staring at a picture of him living his life, doing exactly what he risked everything for. It gave me chills.

I got to see Justin in June when I went to Utah to visit him for a couple of days and then again in July when he and I both flew to North Carolina to visit the family. It was just so good to see him. Justin became such an integral part of who I am when he was sick. I'm sure that sounds silly because he's my son and all of our children play that part in our lives. However, when your child is ill, when you wonder day to day if tomorrow will come for them and when you spend your days praying and hoping and begging for another moment, you become a different kind of "part of each other." I saw it with his siblings as well. Justin symbolized hope and life and love for all of us. We saw him and we knew that anything was possible and miracles really do happen.

CHAPTER 39

In August of 2015 I took a job back in Farmington, New Mexico as a 3rd grade teacher. I was familiar with the area and living there put me about 6 hours from Justin in Provo, Utah. I was kind of lost trying to figure out who I was, where I wanted to live and who I wanted to be so I was drifting in a sense. I sometimes felt like I was wandering around not quite sure where to go or what to do. It would just be me and my little brother close by in New Mexico, as most of my family had moved to North Carolina years before. It would be weird living on my own but being closer to Justin helped as I could visit him often on the weekends. It was unusual because I wasn't a big fan of living in Farmington and I'd finally moved away but then I found myself back. I decided it was temporary. I would teach for the school year and then figure out where I wanted to move.

In mid-August, Justin and his buddies took a guys' trip. Since graduation, it was something they did annually. Justin was finally able to join them. And being the outstanding young men they are, they asked me if I wanted to come too. I went for a day - the day they were climbing a 13,000 foot mountain. It was quite the poetic day. I couldn't help but think about how all of these boys gathered around Justin to conquer cancer and then they were there conquering another mountain together. It was beautiful to see and it was just so fitting.

Things weren't perfect with Justin. There were still struggles and worries and issues. Yes, they were often outweighed by things like hiking 13ers, surfing at the lake and climbing the sheer face of a cliff but they were still there - lurking. Justin's right eye was hemorrhaging pretty badly. He went in to have the blood vessels in that eye cauterized again. The doctor said she was concerned about his retina detaching and him losing sight in that eye. He was scheduled to go back 6 weeks later for more laser surgery but if they couldn't get it under control, they were talking about actual surgery. We were hoping it wouldn't come to that. At some point, I'm sure it's healthy to accept and acknowledge that life would never be the same for Justin and me. That our "normal" would never mesh with the "normal" of most. We would always be worried with every illness, every ache and pain. Every time there was something that stood out, our hearts would drop and we would wait with bated breath until we knew all was okay.

Justin got a full time job, his first ever. What a milestone for him. He was diagnosed when he was 16 so he'd never worked. It was such a joy to listen to him complain about work sometimes. It was one of those rites of passage things, I guess. Life continued on and there we both were doing that living thing. We were both trying to find out who we were. Justin had a great time living with his friends. He'd missed out on that too so it was a big deal for him. He went to concerts and snowboarded. He cleaned the house, walked his dog and went to holiday parties. He was doing exactly what he fought so hard for. Not every day was great for him but he was living every day. He had responsibility thrust on him all at once so to speak and he seemed to handle it well enough. He was able to get frustrated with paying bills and work. He was able to feel the effects of being 21 and having too much to drink on occasion. He experienced what it was like to actually *not* be nauseated. He was living the life of a 21 year old with 3 of his amazing buddies and he put up with, and maybe even enjoyed, my many phone calls and visits.

We all gathered in North Carolina that Christmas of 2015. Back when Justin was so sick, holidays were uncertain. He spent most of them in the hospital. We knew how blessed we were to be able to come together and celebrate our family. I felt as though I had been reminded, in great and painful detail, that life is fragile. I had a better appreciation for time, for moments, for friends and for loved ones because of the journey our family had been on. I think I felt deeper and I tried to soak up every breath with every heartbeat because of it. I thought about how it had truly been my honor and privilege to care for Justin. I got a front row seat to God's grace and mercy.

CHAPTER 40

Deciding to live in New Mexico again, I ran into people pretty regularly who often said, "Wow, I didn't know you were back here. Why in the world did you come back?" Every single time my answer was, "I don't know." I am a firm believer that things happen for a reason - I just never knew what my reason was for being back in New Mexico. In August of the previous year, I just kind of went with it when it happened. Justin was living in Utah and things fell together in such a way for me to stay that I didn't fight it. For a while I thought my reason for being in New Mexico was to be close to Justin. He was only 6 hours away so visiting him often had been easy. He was doing so well and had rocked living on his own and taking care of his health. I finally started to feel like maybe I was coming to understand why I was back. I'm a family person but the majority of my family was in North Carolina with the exception of Justin in Utah and my little brother in New Mexico. So it was basically just me. It was the very first time in my life that I'd essentially been completely on my own. I learned so much about myself, outside of the roles as a mother, daughter and caretaker. I learned about who I was, what I like, what I don't, what's important to me and what isn't. I learned about self-discipline and how to be alone for extended periods of time. I learned how I like to spend my time when it was only me I had to think about. I learned how to do things for me. That was tough. I'd always made decisions based on my kids and my family and that past year I learned how to make decisions just for me. I learned that I'm completely comfortable with myself and time spent with me. After 4 years of being Justin's 24/7 caregiver, which I would gladly do for the rest of my life if he needed it, I think I had to reboot. Going from caring for him completely to not at all was tough and I had to figure who I was after all of that. It's definitely not who I was before. I didn't know if I would stay there after that school year but I did know that the things I'd learned while there would benefit me for a lifetime.

I continued my visits to see Justin, going snowboarding and whatever else we found to get into. In March of 2016, Justin and I flew from our respective towns back to North Carolina for his 5 year post-bone marrow transplant testing. For the most part, he received a good report. However, once back in Utah Justin started feeling terrible. He was running a fever and I felt the effects of living 6 hours away. I didn't know if I should drive up to Utah to see if he was okay. He hadn't been admitted to the hospital in 7 months. I didn't want to overreact but I didn't want to blow it off either. I waited a little bit to see if the fever would increase. It did. I felt a sliver of panic as I threw some clothes in a bag, jumped in my car and began that 6 hour drive. Brady was already on top of it with a plan to head to the house, pick up Justin and drive him to the hospital an hour from where they lived. I was a few hours behind them when all was said and done. Justin was admitted with the flu and another virus. They discharged him the following day only to have to readmit him with an even higher fever, leg pain and severe diarrhea. They did things differently at that hospital and I didn't feel comfortable with Justin there. He was discharged for a second time only to be readmitted several days later. He was still running a fever on and off, throwing up, he had a bad sore throat and a nasty cough. His immune system was struggling to get it kicked. His doctor in Chicago was concerned that his aHUS could start acting up which is what they believe killed his kidneys to begin with. Rotavirus, Parainfluenza A, Rhinovirus and Adenovirus were just a few of the infections that Justin had been diagnosed with. We were still waiting on some test results and a CT scan of his head to come back. No bacterial infections were found but the viruses weren't good either. Justin's immune system was struggling and he felt awful. After receiving some supportive care he was discharged for the 3rd and last time.

The summer of 2016 brought with it more trips to see Justin, Justin's guys' trip, visits to North Carolina to see my family and me moving to Colorado. It also brought a trip for Justin and me back to Durham to have his port removed. It would be the first time in five years that Justin didn't have some sort of device in his body and it marked another enormous milestone for him. As I pulled into the parking garage, as we walked through the underground tunnel, as we took the elevators to remembered floors, saw familiar faces and walked in memorized footsteps, I said to Justin, "I have a lot of feelings." Anyone who knows me knows that comes with the territory. I could feel it all. All of the anxiety, worry and fear I'd had before came rushing back. I felt like I'd been turned inside out and was nothing but raw emotion. I had feelings of anxiousness, nervousness, fear, pain, anger, thankfulness, appreciation and love flood my heart. I felt like a lifetime was crammed into the past five years. We were taken all the way to the edge, as far as you can possibly go without actually going over, and then brought back. I almost felt like Justin was being released from the grip cancer held on him for so long. It felt like he was breaking free. I watched him sleep so many times, sometimes with fear he wouldn't wake up. To look at him that day and to know that he made such a turnaround is what I'd tirelessly hoped and prayed for.

At the end of the summer Justin had his 22nd birthday. Sometimes I was honestly lost for words. When my phone rang and I saw his face pop on the screen, when I got to hear his voice and hug his neck - I thanked God that he was still here to celebrate another year of life.

That same summer I began having bad knee issues. I went to a doctor in Colorado in August and found out that I had complete patellar instability along with some messed up cartilage. The doctor wanted to operate and perform the Fulkerson procedure so I scheduled a time for September. He told me that with 6-8 months of physical therapy I should be back to good. I was bummed that I would miss out on snowboarding that upcoming winter but with all of the pain and swelling I knew I had to get it taken care of. I had the surgery on September 7th, 2016 and Justin and his friends came to move me back to Farmington on September 10th. Things had changed in Colorado and I'd come to the final decision to move back to North Carolina by way of New Mexico. Justin was doing well and I decided that if he needed anything I could fly to wherever he was. However, I would have to wait a couple of months to move because of the surgery I'd just had. My little brother, Kevin, let me stay with him until I felt strong enough to make the drive back to North Carolina. Life kept changing. It felt like I was in a push and pull, trying to find a place I fit.

CHAPTER 41

There I was making plans again and God had something, or rather someone, altogether different in mind. Being back in Farmington, I spent a lot of time with my brother and his family. They were always so gracious. Nevertheless, I was going a little stir crazy. I started hanging out occasionally with a friend, Eddie. I'd met him about a year before and we always enjoyed each other's company. He was funny and it was relaxing to be around him. He put up with having to baby my leg, helping me into and out of the car as well as booths at restaurants. He was a great sport and I was grateful for time with him. A friendship that began with shared interests and the enjoyment of being around each other quickly grew into something more and I wasn't quite prepared.

I continued my trips to see Justin, this time in the passenger seat. And Justin continued his check-ups at the doctor. His eye continued to be an issue. And then there was an even bigger issue that emerged. Justin's labs started looking questionable - specifically his urine and his creatinine. They were seeing high levels of both white and red blood cells in his urine and upon further testing and inspection said they saw "cells they can't identify." That was a familiar phrase that took me back to the beginning when Justin was first diagnosed with leukemia. The hospital in Chicago received the reports from Salt Lake City and called wanting a scope of Justin's bladder. Our biggest fear was that the dreaded BK Virus was back. To add a bit more worry his creatinine was the highest it had been since transplant, indicating that his kidney may not be working right. He was chugging water in the hopes that it was just dehydration. We scheduled him for a bladder biopsy and a cystoscopy the following week in Chicago. Justin and I talked about how long it had been since we felt that level of worry and panic. We almost forgot what it tasted like.

He had labs first thing the morning of his scope. Then he had a bladder scope around 8:00 AM. The results of the bladder scope left my heart in my stomach. They saw a tumor in his bladder and before I knew it he was scheduled for surgery the following day to remove as much as they could of the tumor and send it for biopsy. We both thought the tumor was related to BK Virus – similar to what he had before. He had such hell with that for so long when he was in Durham and it was one of the things the doctors worried about after kidney transplant. My mind raced as I contemplated what that could mean. Based on his scope results, everything changed for the day. Justin was sent for an MRI to see if there were any other concerns. He also had some pre-op testing to be sure he was medically okay for surgery. They postponed his kidney biopsy because they were concerned with it bleeding and interfering with the bladder surgery.

The urologist sat down beside me in the waiting room after a surgery that took much longer than expected. "Bladder cancer - I'm nearly positive it's bladder cancer. Of course we will wait for pathology to confirm but I've seen it too many times." They thought they got it all. They were going to do a chemo wash in his bladder until they realized that it would hurt his transplanted kidney. And then the doctor was gone. I stared out the window right in front of me and felt a hot, wet tear slip down my cheek, and then another. Within seconds I was in a full blown cry. I couldn't believe that Justin had cancer again. I wouldn't believe it. I replayed the doctor's words in my head just to be sure I heard him right. I couldn't have. I made myself think of all of the other things it could have been. There were a few times the past 5 years that I felt like I was watching myself from the outside. I saw myself sitting in this chair in a hospital in Chicago. I saw all of the other people in that waiting room with stories of their own. None of them saw my pain. None of them could understand it if they had.

Does doing something more than once make it easier? I methodically touched the numbers in my phone that coincided with Eddie's phone. I needed him to tell me that everything was fine. I needed him to reassure me that it was a mistake. Mostly, I just needed to hear his voice. Then I called Jason and the rest of my family to let everyone know the current status. Minutes later the nurse came to get me. It was time to go see Justin in recovery and I was left staring at a door that I had to find the strength to walk through and tell my son for the second time that he may have cancer. How does someone do that? You would think that it may be easier the second time around. You would think that with experience, maybe it wouldn't sting as much. Or maybe defenses would be prepared to "handle" the news. That wasn't the case. I walked into Justin's recovery room and he groggily looked over at me as I entered. I waited a while until some of the medication wore off. I started to tell him what Dr. Johnson, the urologist, shared with me but he'd already told him. Justin immediately said he wouldn't do chemo again. I asked him to please just wait for us to get more information – to not make any decisions yet. After all, we weren't even positive it was cancer. He said that was fine but the bottom line is he wouldn't do chemo again, he just wouldn't. It stung my heart because I knew what that meant. I knew that if he *did* have cancer he would more likely have to have chemo and if he was refusing, well…he probably wouldn't have a chance. But how could I blame him after what he'd gone through before with chemo? How could I ask him to do it again? We plodded out of the hospital and into a taxi to take us back to the hotel. We were done. We were spent. We fell into our beds back at the hotel, emotionally exhausted. We didn't talk but we didn't sleep either. I think we were both lost in our own heads. I wondered what was going on in his but I didn't ask because I honestly didn't know what to say.

Justin went home to Provo and I went to Farmington. And we waited.

CHAPTER 42

I had the personal phone numbers of both Dr. Starnes (Justin's nephrologist) and Dr. Johnson (Justin's urologist) in Chicago. Even though Dr. Starnes wasn't in charge of the bladder portion of all of this, he was kind enough to keep us updated with current information. Needless to say I text both doctors daily asking if the pathology results were back. I reasoned with myself and with God. I tried to find all of the reasons it would be impossible for Justin to have cancer again. It was a way to comfort myself, I guess.

I was lying on the couch, my head in Eddie's lap, watching TV when my phone beeped with that familiar ding of a text. My phone was at my feet, plugged into the wall charging. Worried, I sat up slowly with my back to Eddie and read the text from Justin's doctor: "It *is* a cancer. Not typical bladder cancer." The text went on to say that someone would call me the following day. I shook as I sobbed and Eddie rubbed my back trying to comfort my terrified mind and heart, not knowing exactly what he could possibly say. I had truly made myself believe it couldn't have been cancer. We were both finally acclimating to life outside of the hospitals. It was cruel.

I called Justin immediately. It's so much harder to deliver news like that over the phone, without being able to reach out and hold him to reassure him that we would figure it out. We had before and we would again. He sounded so dejected when I told him. He was quiet and what scared me the most was that when he spoke it almost, for a very brief moment, sounded like he had given up – like he conceded. He had been knocked on his ass. He'd come so far and it was insane that he would be diagnosed with a second cancer. I told him how very much I loved him, that we would figure it out as we had before and then we hung up. His best friend and roommate called me moments later asking what he could do. I

177

told him how worried I was about Justin's state of mind and asked him if he could take him to do something fun. In good Brady fashion he said he was already on it as they were headed out to ride go-karts.

All I could do was stare at the space, the moment, directly in front of me. It's an odd feeling to literally try to wrap your head around news like that. I could feel my mind turning over the past 5 years of hospital stays, procedures, chemo, radiation, medications and the like in the search for something that made sense. I could feel my mind stretch, my thoughts racing, searching for something. My head spun, my thoughts jumbled and confused. There was a familiar gnawing at the back of my brain and a recognized weight in my gut. God had been using Justin for a long while for His works. I just didn't feel like He was finished yet. People told me to pray and that everything would be okay. Having traveled that road before and having prayed unceasingly the first time, I knew that wasn't the case. Just because we prayed or felt that things would be okay didn't mean that getting to that point wouldn't be tough. And what does "okay" mean anyway? It's relative.

I looked directly at the space in front of me and I asked myself what I needed to do in that moment, for that space of time. And I continued do so with each moment after. Because sometimes all you can do is breathe and think about only the second in front of you. And that's how you get through. I hoped.

It felt like Justin had fought the valiant fight. He fought so hard for so long. It reminded me of when he played baseball. Those 9 innings could be tough but the players were *given* those 9 innings to prove themselves. Those 9 innings were an automatic, unless they gave up early on and were run-ruled. It was in the 10th inning that the guts of the players changed. It was then that they had to reach down deep to show what they were really made of and how much they really wanted that win. It was the 10th inning, that extra inning, that they had to leave it all out on the field and know they did their best, whatever the outcome. Justin had many 10th innings. The first one began a couple of weeks after his diagnosis. He asked me then what it would mean if he just stopped – if he allowed the cancer to dictate the outcome. Since then he has had to fight it out in many 10th innings. He's had to dig deep and uncover a strength within himself that even he didn't know he possessed. And that is exactly what he would do again.

We went back to Chicago on November 1st to the cancer center to discuss options for Justin. The oncologist talked to us about removing Justin's bladder completely and making him a new one (could we not?). She also mentioned removing part of his bladder and then having him return every 3-6 months to have it biopsied. The latter sounded much more desirable and do-able. She discussed with us the rarity of Justin getting that cancer and where he had it. That didn't faze us. We lived the past 5 years with that explanation. She left the room and I looked at Justin sitting on that beige colored, bland examining table. The white paper was pulled down the middle and when we left I knew they would pull that paper down, tear it off and wait for the next patient. I wondered how many parents and their children sat in the respective seats we were sitting in. I wondered what ran through their heads and I wondered if their heart ever felt like it would stop beating the way mine did. I didn't say anything at first. I just tried to sift through my own thoughts before trying to explore Justin's. We opted for the second plan and scheduled surgery on Dec. 1st.

Sometimes in the midst of pain and worry, God hands you a gift; light for the way and ease for your worries. Sometimes between the tears and the fear, you experience more love and life than in a million trouble-free moments strung together. And the best part is that life's simple joys mean everything to you. Things that we once took for granted became so incredibly significant. I had no idea how in the world we were back in that familiar place. I didn't know why God decided that Justin wasn't quite done with this battle with cancer but I'm thankful for the love, happiness and joy that we experienced despite the sound of our breaking hearts. There was a peace almost, a calm in the middle of the storm that Justin was asked to walk through again. I can't quite explain it. Justin stood up and decided he would take the punches and then he would give a few of his own with God's will.

Jenna met up with Justin, Jason and me in Chicago for Justin's surgery. When we all arrived, we pensively just looked at each other for a while. I know we were all wondering the same thing, asking all the same questions in that silent place in our hearts. The following day we trudged back into that hospital in Chicago that 2 years previously gave Justin a new lease on life. We weren't sure what to expect. Justin's other cancer was a blood cancer and this was a tumor. We were in uncharted waters again. We arrived at the hospital early in the morning and Justin was the first to be called back. As always we stayed with Justin in pre-op until they made us leave and then we headed out to the waiting room. We were there for what felt like an unusually long time, entertaining ourselves and trying not to think about what we were all surely thinking about. We were in the waiting room literally the entire day. Justin's surgery lasted about 3 hours but it took a lot longer to get him into a room. The doctor removed part of his bladder and took biopsies of his lymph nodes. They left in a catheter that Justin would have to keep for 10 days to relieve pressure on his bladder. That evening Justin finally got a room and we all went to check on him. He was in some pain but doing well. They wanted to keep him for a couple of days to be sure that his bladder would drain okay and that there weren't any leaks. We spent the next couple of days walking around the hospital, as the doctors instructed. Justin seemed to be healing fine. After he healed completely from the surgery, the doctors would reassess to see if he would need chemo and/or radiation or even another surgery. After Justin's discharge we stayed in Chicago for a few days and then flew home. We decided to get Justin's catheter removed back home in Farmington.

A few days later his doctor called. He said that the pathology came back negative so there were no more traces of cancer cells in his bladder and the lymph nodes tested negative so it hadn't spread. He was going to talk to the oncologist that week about next steps, but he felt like we would have to go back to Chicago once every three months. He didn't think Justin would need anything more than that. The oncologist was tossing around the idea of a round or two of chemo but the doctor didn't think it would be necessary. And Justin had already made up his mind about that.

We finally heard from Dr. Johnson in Chicago who told us that Justin would have to be seen in Chicago every 3 months for the first 2 years, then every 6 months for 10 years and then annually forever, for a cystoscopy and other testing. That didn't include his transplant labs, eye appointments, kidney transplant follow up and annual bone marrow transplant evaluations that he would continue to have. The cancer may be gone but his fight wasn't over.

Justin decided to come live with Eddie and me in Farmington for a while. He'd decided that he wanted to go a different direction with his life and felt that he could really focus on healing his mind, heart and body in Farmington. We had to run it by the doctors in Chicago since he was supposed to be living near a transplant hospital. They gave us the go ahead – for now. After all that had happened, I was happy that he would be close for a while. He discussed working out to get his body healthy again and in doing so, his mind. He also decided he wanted to go to college. I was proud of him and I was thankful. We don't know God's plans but we discovered how to live in those moments in between and that's what we intended to do. We were the lucky ones. In the years of watching Justin fight to survive, we learned how to really live.

CHAPTER 43

Life is funny. It can force you into change with various dynamics. It can take you to the absolute edge and push against you as you claw your way back. And it can show you the beauty in the midst of the most devastating pain. God gave us exactly who we needed to make it through our journey. We don't know what tomorrow holds but we have hope that it will be beautiful and bright.

So here's to taking chances and laughing at the odds. Here's to sunsets on mountain tops, laughter on the side of the road with the best people we know and the excitement of sunrises to come. Here's to the paths less traveled and the friends we meet along the way. Here's to answered prayers and the moments we never saw coming. Here's to the places we've gone and the many adventures waiting ahead. Here's to right now...

(Latin) Cum omnis spiritus, spero-- which translates into, "With every breath, I hope."

Works Cited:

1. Leukemia & Lymphoma Society,
   htpps://www.lls.org/managing-your-cancer/lab-and-imaging-tests/blood-tests. April 20, 2017.

2. *Wikipedia.*
   https://en.m.wikipedia.org/wiki/hypodiploid_acute_lymphoblastic_leukemia. April 20, 2017.

3. *bethematch.org.* Be the Match,
   https://bethematch.org/transplant-basics/matching-patients-with-donors/how-donors-and-patients-are-matche/hla-basics. April 20, 2017.

4. *WebMD.* WebMD,
   https://www.webmd.com/a-to-z-guides/neutropenia-causes-symptoms-treatment. November 11, 2017.

5. *medicinenet.com.* Medicinenet,
   https://www.medicinenet.com/script/main/mobileart.asp?articlekey=12550. May 1, 2016.

6. Neutropenia.ca. The Neutropenia
   Association , 1993,
   http://www.neutropenia.ca/about/what-is-neutropenia. March 3, 2016.

7. *WebMD.* WebMD,
   https://www.webmd.com/a-to-z-guides/foot-drop-causes-symptoms-treatments. August 20, 2017.

8. *Cancerquest.org.* Cancerquest,
   https://www.cancerquest.org/patients/treatments/bone-marrow-transplantation#7. December 10, 2016.

9. Bill Biermann. *Ning.com.* aHUS
   Foundation,
   https://atypicalhus.ning.com/page/what-is-ahus. January 11, 2017.

10. *WebMD.* WebMD,

https://webmd.com/multiple-sclerosis/plasma-exchange-ms. September 15, 2017.

11. *MedicinePlus*. Medicine Plus, https://medicineplus.gov/ency/article007305.htm. November 11, 2017.

12. *WebMD*. WebMD, August 27, 2015.

13. Nplate.com. Nplate, www.nplate.com/patient/about-nplate/index/. August 16, 2015.

14. Sciencedirect.com. Sciencedirect, www.sciencedirect.com/topics/medicine-and-dentistry/bilevel-positive-airway-pressure. June 202, 2016.

15. WebMD. WebMD, www.webmd.com/a-to-z-guides/hyperkalemia-causes-sypmtoms-treatments#1. October 2, 2015

16. *Marrow Forums*. Marrow Forums, http://forums.marrowforums.org/showthread.php?t=1361. November 10, 2017.

17. *WebMD*. WebMD, https://www.webmd.com/skin-problems-and-treatments/mrsa-directory. October 16, 2015

18. *Hopkinsmedicine.org*. Hopkins Medicine, https://www.hopkinsmedicine.org/kimmel_cancer_center/bone_marrow_transplant/haploididentical_transplantation.html. November 11, 2017

19. *Wikipedia*. Wikipedia, https://en.m.wikipedia.org/wiki/Panel_reactive_antibody. September 15, 2017.

20. *WebMD*. WebMD, https://www.webmd.com/a-to-z-guides/tc/organ-transplant-preparing-for-a-transplant-2. October 24, 2013

21. *Hormone.org*. Hormone Health Network,

https://www.hormone.org/hormones-and-health/the-endocrine-system/adrenal-glands. February 12, 2015

ABOUT THE AUTHOR

Jennifer Staley is a school teacher turned momma to a cancer kid. She was a photojournalist for 4 years for an off-road magazine and always hoped to write a book someday. Jennifer imagined it would be a children's book but life thrust her in a different direction. Years of street education and endless hour of research has culminated in the creation of this treasure. Her hope is that after you read this, after you see the devastating effects that cancer has on children, after you witness the acute pain and suffering that you will encourage others to see it too. Help others listen to the pleas of the children and families devastated by this disease. And if you *are* one of the families affected by childhood cancer, know there is hope.

Made in the USA
San Bernardino, CA
09 December 2017